Edgar Cayce on
The Mysterious Essenes

Edgar Cayce on
The Mysterious Essenes

Lessons from Our Sacred Past

John Van Auken
Ruben Miller, PhD

A.R.E. Press • Virginia Beach • Virginia

A.R.E. Press
215 67th Street
Virginia Beach, VA 23451-2061

ISBN 13: 978-0-87604-866-5

John's biblical quotes come from *The World English Bible* which is a 1997 revision of the American Standard Version of the Holy Bible, first published in 1901. It is found on the web and is in the Public Domain.

Cover design by Christine Fulcher

CONTENTS

Introduction
Ruben Miller

The idea for this book began when I was reflecting on the Norfolk, Virginia study group and how all of these people back in 1930–31 got together with Hugh Lynn, Edgar Cayce's eldest son, and how they formed the new Association for Research and Enlightenment (A.R.E.). And I got to thinking about something that Eula Allen (the author of Cayce books: *Before the Beginning*, *The River of Time*, and *You Are Forever*) once said to Hannah Miller and me, "We are the *same* people that were back in those days, and we are here again." We are those Essenes who have come back in a group at the A.R.E. This is what made me keep thinking about the Essenes. The more I thought about it, the more I felt it would be wonderful to have a book to give the background of why they started. We are the Essenes, and we are doing those same things we did back then. It may be in a different way, but we are doing the same things. And we still have the soul of Edgar Cayce to help us with his readings. He was one of those who was also incarnate during the time of the Essenes as Lucius.

In 2014 I was at the A.R.E. headquarters for the annual Congress of Members in Virginia Beach, Virginia and shared my idea with writer

John Van Auken. He immediately liked my premise and agreed to join me in writing this fascinating topic: the reincarnation of the Essenes.

John flew down to my home in south Florida, turned on his recorder, and listened as I began to share my many years of working with these people whose souls Edgar Cayce had identified as reincarnated Essenes. Some of whom were my dearest friends. I had never heard of the Essenes before Cayce. And the more I heard about the Essenes and knew them personally, the more I felt this book had to be written.

The stories are truly amazing. For example, Judy Chandler was alive when I came to help the Association. She worked for the government in Washington, DC at that time. She came down to headquarters a couple of times, and that's when I met her. She was an elderly lady then and was very ill. Hugh Lynn asked us to pray for her because she was suffering. I learned that she had been an Essene teacher and that she had actually taught the boy Jesus in the Essene school on Mount Carmel! And here I was praying for her well-being in this lifetime! "Oh yes," I told John, "We can have a whole chapter on her!"

I thought this book would be a wonderful way of explaining to most people about their souls' lives, where their souls have been, and how they return to complete what their souls started.

I was a newcomer in the Norfolk study group. We mostly talked about the Bible. Noah Miller could bring the Bible alive. We studied Genesis for about seven years. He made that book come alive! And you know, I used to tell Mom and Pop about these things and they would say, "You have your God and we have ours." So I brought Papa a New Testament written in Yiddish. He would read that every night at dinner and he couldn't believe what he was reading. Well, Jesus was a Jew. Yes, he was. But Papa also came from Russia, so he wasn't accustomed to this. And his mother lived with us, so we were very Orthodox. To this day, I don't eat meat and milk together, or butter and meat together, or a hamburger with cheese on it—no dairy and meat. I don't mix the two, never have in my entire life. So I'm still Orthodox—a little bit.

Ruth Denney had been told by Cayce that her soul was the reincarnation of Josie. Josie was a nurse and she had a grandson. When Ruth was in the hospital dying, she told me that I was that grandson of hers in the time of the Essenes. She died about two years after I knew her. She said the reason why she came to me is that she recognized me as her grandson from Bethlehem when she was Josie. That's what brought me into the A.R.E. I never thought about that. I just put it out of my mind as it never meant that much. It was the same as when Hugh Lynn and I were in Israel in front of the Billy Rose Museum, sitting on those stone stoops, and Hugh Lynn said, "You know, Ruben, you were the Jew my father spoke about." That Jew was supposed to be the necessary ingredient in the new Association succeeding. Me. I didn't believe it. But now, these many years later, maybe it's true. I do love the Edgar Cayce readings and many of the people I've met through this organization. It has meant so much to my life.

I hope you will find this material as interesting and helpful as I have.

Chapter 1

Reincarnation of
Soul Groups

This is a book about reincarnation, specifically the reincarnation of a group of souls who were once known as the Essenes. It is also about souls *associated* with the Essenes, their origin, eventual establishment, and their legacy. And it is also about souls today who carry in their hearts and minds the principles and mission of the Essenes.

In some respects souls are like rivers—on the surface they are all shiny and clear, shimmering with freshness and life, but deep beneath the surface run powerful unseen currents which influence the outer incarnate self and its relationships with other souls. These influences make for attractions and repulsions. And since souls are immortal, their physical bodies age and die but they, their souls, do not. They carry on, both in this physical world and beyond. Our soul is of God, made in the image of God (Genesis 1:26), and only the outer *persona* is temporarily living as a terrestrial physical being for as long as the physical body remains animated with the life forces. The deep currents of the unseen nonphysical self bring influences into this life and personality from cumulative ages of soul-life which consist of both incarnate lives in earth and discarnate sojourns beyond earth. These deeper influences are the cause for our easy love and patience with one person while having impatience and dislike for another. These undercurrents cause us to feel wonderful vibrations with a particular individual in one aspect of our lives only to feel awkward and uncomfortable with that same person in another aspect of our lives. For example, we would naturally have a warm comfort and attraction to a soul with whom we had been a sibling in a previous incarnation but quite uncomfortable with him or her in a sexual setting. Dynamics of relating with one another on a soul level have been formed deep within our inner consciousness, and they shape the way we innately interact with one another and situations in this present incarnation. Most everyone in our present life was very likely in one or more of our past lives. Souls that are very close to us in this life were likely involved in *many* of our past lives. Our parents, brothers and sisters, spouses, children, friends, colleagues, bosses and employees, and even those we dislike were involved in our past lives. Again, on the surface they have new faces, freshly developing personalities, and likely new roles, but beneath that shiny surface runs currents of lengthy times together carrying their often unconscious influences.

The effects of these many past-life experiences are reflected in the circumstances that now surround our present situations and relationships. This is karma. Our soul's memories of past-life activities with others shape innate reaction to them today. Of course, *their* memories of our past-life actions influence how they react to us. Through the same eyes that the personality sees life, the soul sees it, but the soul looks with a memory covering ages of passion and adventure, care and love, hatred and revenge, doubt and fear, hopes and disappointments. When we feel a seemingly unfounded fondness for a person, it is very likely due to soul memory of the positive role he or she played in our past lives. On the other hand, when we react with what seems to be an unfounded dislike or even revulsion, possibly even hatred, we can be pretty sure it is because our soul recalls how harmful they were to us or those we loved.

However, the influences of past-life actions are not always so clear. Often those with whom we have had good lives and relationships are the same people with whom we have had problems and disagreements. There is usually a mixture of good and bad karma influencing us today.

Those positive, well-developed aspects from our past lives will give us much pleasure and support in the present. Conversely, those aspects that were not positive will challenge us today, causing us to struggle to resolve the lingering disharmony. Avoiding these influences is simply not possible. Whether we like it or not, the Universal Law of Karma flows through us with the currents of *unresolved issues* that force us to greet the boomerang of past actions, thoughts, feelings, and words spoken. Thus, what we have done to other souls and they have done to us is reflected in the circumstances surrounding our present relationships and the innate urges, attitudes, and emotions we feel toward each other—*and how we feel about ourselves internally*. Much of our self-judgment is the karmic result of how we've used our free will prior to this lifetime. And no one can change that perspective *except us!* That is why we reincarnate. Each lifetime is an opportunity for resolution and soul growth which includes learning about ourselves, others, and the God-force running throughout life. "Live and learn" is the theme.

These basic ideas of past relationships and their present influences are not only true of individual relationships but also of *group* relationships. From the beginning souls have traveled together in *groups*, and the very act of traveling together for such long periods creates forces of attraction and repulsion that reinforce the group dynamics. Nearly all souls on the planet today were together in past ages of human history. As a result, the relationships among the peoples of the world today are a reflection of their past activities. In fact, Edgar Cayce points to a verse in the scriptures that reveals who we are and how we once traveled together as one single, massive soul group: "When the Morning Stars sang together and all the children of God shouted for joy!" (Job 38:7) Cayce teaches that all souls associated with this dimension of life were those Morning Stars traveling from out of the heavens into this realm of physical existence, joyfully ready to live and learn. At that time we were in harmony, of one mind, and intimately connected to one another in a collective consciousness. We moved as a group, not as individuals, like a flock of birds, like a school of fish. Cayce teaches that as we gradually descended into matter and physicality, we became more *individualized*. Eventually it came to the point to where each soul had its own separate body, completely individualized. This reduced the sense of togetherness, connectedness, and *belonging*. Yet, even in this materialized condition, there remain some smaller group dynamic to which we considered ourselves to be a part of—this family, this neighborhood, this race, this faith, this culture, and so on. But now it was with a profoundly individualized self. And this was a natural flow of life. From the moment we were conceived, we have been driven to know ourselves to be ourselves and yet somehow retain the sense of our belonging to the Whole of beings and life. Oneness with all life is an innate feeling that surfaces in souls who become even slightly enlivened or enlightened.

The soul-group journey is neither simple nor homogeneous. Souls who came in to this planetary system and entered the realms of consciousness associated with this region of the universe comprise our largest soul group: The Morning Stars. This group can then be divided into the subgroups we call "the generations," containing souls who move through the natural cycles of Earth life together, and can then be further divided into the various nations, cultures, races, religions, and so on. Within these groups are the subgroups of souls which share similar philosophies, ideals, purposes, aspirations, and attitudes. From here the soul groups further divide into the many smaller groups of personal relationships: communities, families, businesses, teams, schools, and so on.

Soul groups create an affinity among their members not only by the cumulative experiences they share, but also through their *collective* memory of how life has been for them and what they mutually desire and detest. In a manner of speaking, such groups form a distinct *collective consciousness* and spirit, much like the souls who gave us "the spirit of '76" that led to the founding of the United States of America in 1776. This spirit reflected that soul group's *mutual* hopes, attitudes, purposes, and memories. And as we all know from history, they had *differing* individual ideas about how best to form a new nation, but they were nevertheless in harmony on the *ideal!* Thus, they worked through their differences for the sake of the ideal: a nation that could allow for differences while maintaining a collective unity. They stated this in their declaration: "We hold these truths to be self-evident, that all men are created equal, that they are endowed by their Creator with certain unalienable rights, that among these are Life, Liberty and the pursuit of Happiness." And stated it again in the preamble to their constitution: "We the People of the

United States, in Order to form a more perfect union, establish Justice, insure domestic tranquility, provide for the common defense, promote the general welfare, and secure the blessings of liberty to ourselves and our posterity, do ordain and establish this Constitution for the United States of America." These words reflect a soul group's collective consciousness that binds them into a distinct group while allowing for individual differences.

It is important to keep in mind that soul groups are neither rigid nor static. Any individual soul can use its free will to seek an experience with another group. There are many cases of souls changing political allegiance, race, or religion from one lifetime to another. Neither do the generations incarnate in strict, rigid patterns. A member of one generation may enter again with a different generation. For example, two members of a family group who were father and son in one life may change positions and become grandfather and grandson. They may also choose not to be in the same family. Thus, amid the predominant flow of the undercurrents of the collective there remains a degree of individual freedom.

Although soul groups are fairly well established and have significant pull on the individuals in them, they do *not* have greater influence than an individual soul's free will. That is the great individualizing power given by the Creative Forces that conceived souls. Each soul has the inner power to determine its own way. It simply has to understand that its choices have reactions, consequences, and outcomes—its karma.

Generally, however, soul groups cycle in and out of the earth together and, therefore, at approximately the same time. (I am speaking in eras and ages, not days or years.) This is particularly evident in Edgar Cayce's past-life "readings," as they are called. Many of these past-life readings were for souls who fell into one of two major soul groups and naturally followed their group's cycles of incarnating. Edgar Cayce and those who worked closely with him also traveled with one of these two groups. Gina Cerminara, author of one of the best books on Edgar Cayce's past-life perspective, entitled *Many Mansions*, researched Cayce's past-life readings and developed these lists.

The Cycle of Incarnations of Two Soul Groups

Group 1:
> Early Atlantis
> Early Ancient Egypt
> Persia (during the time of Croesus, king of Lydia)
> Palestine (during the time of Jesus)
> The Crusades
> Colonial America

Group 2:
> Late Atlantis
> Late Ancient Egypt
> Early Greece
> Rome (during the time of Jesus)
> France (during the time of Louis XIV, XV, XVI)
> The American Civil War

Of course, these are only the most significant incarnations for these souls; they likely had more incarnations than the lists indicate. There were also other incarnation sequences given, but the majority of the readings were for souls who typically cycled with one of these two major groups. We should also take a look at some significant exceptions to this pattern. Some souls did not always incarnate with their group, choosing instead to skip a cycle or enter with another group, though they usually *rejoined* their primary group eventually. Others, though cycling into the earth plane with their group, did not actually incarnate; they did not enter into a body; they rather stayed in the spirit and helped from a higher vantage point those who were incarnated. One example of this comes from an Edgar Cayce reading for a woman who wanted to know why she hadn't been given an incarnation during the Palestine era in which her present son and husband had incarnated. She was told that she was indeed involved in those activities but not in a physical body (incarnate). She was, as some of us would term it today, a "guardian angel" for her present son while he lived and worked in that period. And if she hadn't done this, he would have fallen off the good path several times!

A group of souls may find themselves together again and yet not one of them desired it to be so. In these cases, it is often the forces of the Universal Law of Karma that compels them to come together. For better or for worse they now have to meet the effects of past actions with each other. The intention is that the confrontation will lead to a resolution of their karma or at least to a recognition of how past actions with each other have caused the present predicament, and hopefully then they will use their free wills to dissolve the karmic influence.

Both in individual and group relationships, the karmic effects of past actions with others can create some very difficult, even terrible situations. The meeting can result in murder, rape, torture, and other atrocities. Even in lesser cases karmic reactions can result in backbiting, backstabbing, bickering, contention, fighting, and turmoil. Imagine what might happen if the universal forces of cause and effect brought together the souls of the gladiators of the Roman Colosseum and the souls they had fed to the lions, or the Conquistadors and the Aztecs, or the Nazis and the Jews.

The same cause–and–effect forces play a part in individual lives too. Imagine if the law of karma brought together the murderer and victim killed in a family quarrel. What about a soul who betrayed another's trust or love? What would be the reaction toward one another in this present life? Imagine the dynamics of working with someone who once tortured you or your loved ones. Imagine if you had tortured him or her and her loved ones. Imagine if you were publicly humiliated and burned at the stake. What would be your emotions upon meeting those people today? When lives are heavily burdened by the negative effects of their past actions, their present experience is often horrid, even tragic, and occasionally their lives may appear to be wasted senselessly. However, from the soul's perspective a single incarnation is a learning experience and an opportunity to resolve past actions that are holding the soul back from its growth and ultimate destiny. One physical life is not the ultimate living experience for an *immortal* soul. It is an op-portunity to resolve the burdens that past actions have upon us. It is an opportunity to clear away the many ideas that continue to confuse and mislead us. It's an opportunity to break habit patterns that possess us and limit our ability to grow. Even though the eighty to a hundred years that comprise the average lifetime seems so very singular and final to the outer portion of our being, it is only a temporary sojourn, a brief experience along an infinite path of soul–life.

Of course, all the *good* that has been experienced among the various souls and soul groups has just as strong an effect on present situations as does the bad. And when we focus on this "good karma," we often find better ways to resolve the negative.

This book looks at one distinct soul group that we call today the Essenes. It deals with how they began to bond together *long before* the incarnation of their group and how they are continuing to affect thoughts and actions today.

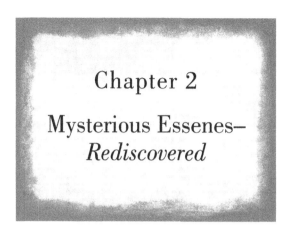

Chapter 2
Mysterious Essenes–
Rediscovered

It was a surprise to everyone present when the so-called "Sleeping Prophet," Edgar Cayce, began giving a trance-state discourse about a soul group called the Essenes (pronounced, *es-scenes*), stating that they played a major role in the *spiritual* journey of humankind. Except for a few scholars and ancient-history buffs, no one on the planet had heard of the Essenes—that is until 1947 when the Dead Sea Scrolls were discovered in caves in Qumran. And that discovery occurred two years *after* Cayce's death in 1945, so he was teaching about a group that had not yet been discovered—revealing more about the so-called "Akashic record" and how all is recorded on this etheric film, this "collective mind," and can be read if one's own mind can tune into it, as Cayce's did.

The *physical* Dead Sea Scrolls were found north of legendary Masada, along the northwestern shore of the Dead Sea. And though the Bible mentions Pharisees and Sadducees, it does not mention Essenes by name. Yet, we now know that the Essenes were deeply involved in Jewish and early Christian activities.

Historical records of the Essenes have given us some insight into this mysterious soul group, who were sometimes called Nazarenes, having originally come from Nazareth. The primary historical sources containing information about the Essenes are from these classical writers and their documents:

- Flavius Josephus: *The Wars of the Jews* (ca. 75CE), *The Antiquities of the Jews* (ca. 94CE), and *The Life of Flavius Josephus* (ca. 97CE).
- Philo Judaeus (ca. 20–54CE): *Quod Omnis Probus Liber, Hypothetica* in Eusebius, *Praeparatio Evangelica*, and *De Vita Contemplativa*.
- Pliny the Elder (died ca. 79CE): *Natural History*.
- Epiphanius of Salamis: *Panarion* (ca. 378CE).

According to these records, the Essenes were a large group of serious spiritual seekers, and though their scrolls were found in Qumran, their headquarters was on Mount Carmel. (Epiphanius of Salamis, *Panarion* 1:18, and Josephus, *The Wars of the Jews*)

Mount Carmel is a coastal mountain range, twenty-four miles long, in northern Israel in the hills of Galilee and the Golan Heights, overlooking the Mediterranean Sea. There are many caves in this mountain range as well as lush vegetation, making it a historically ideal place for those seeking refuge from the authorities or the general population. In the Book of Amos, a prophetic book of the Hebrew Bible, Mount Carmel was a place of refuge for Elijah and Elisha. (Amos 9:3) The biblical Book of Kings states that an altar to God was built on this mount in ancient times and Elijah rebuilt that altar during his time. (II Kings 2:25) And it was at this altar that Elijah challenged four hundred and fifty priests of Baal to a contest to prove whose god was the one true God. (I Kings 18:19–46) In the story, the Baal priests could not get their god to respond to their pleas, but Elijah's prayers brought fire down upon the altar and much needed rain to the mount. Even as far back as the 1400s BCE, Egyptian Pharaoh Thutmose III considered the mount to be a holy site in the Canaanite territories! (Cheyne and Black, *Encyclopedia Biblica*) Pythagoras actually visited the mountain and considered it to be one of the most holy of all mountains. According to Roman historian Tacitus, there was an oracle on Mount Carmel that Emperor Vespasian consulted during his reign. Tacitus also confirmed that there was an altar there—an altar that had no images and did not have a temple around it. (*Jewish Encyclopedia*: "Carmel, Mount")

According to Edgar Cayce (254-109), the Essenes were the continuation of the legendary "School of the Prophets" begun by the High Priest

Melchizedek, who broke bread and drank wine with Abraham (Genesis 14:18). The school was further developed by the prophet Samuel around 1020 BCE in Ramah, a town about four miles northwest of Jerusalem. (I Samuel 19:18-24) And this school was revived by Elijah on Mount Carmel around 860 BCE.

In the Bible there are over twenty mentions of the School of the Prophets and groups of prophets working together. Here are a few key ones: In 1 Samuel 19:19-24 we have, "Then Saul sent messengers to take David, but when they [the messengers] saw the company of the prophets prophesying, with Samuel standing and presiding over them, the Spirit of God came upon the messengers of Saul; and they also prophesied. When it was told to Saul, he sent other messengers, and they also prophesied. So Saul sent messengers again the third time, and they also prophesied." Later in chapter 10:5-6 we find this, "Samuel said to Saul, 'Tell the servant to pass on before us, and when he has passed on stop here yourself for a while, that I may make known to you the word of God. [Samuel then said] You will come to the hill of God where the Philistine garrison is; and it shall be as soon as you have come there to the city, that you will meet a group of prophets coming down from the high place with harp, tambourine, flute, and a lyre before them, and they will be prophesying. Then the Spirit of the Lord will come upon you mightily, and you shall prophesy with them and be changed into another man.'" In Ezra 5:2 we have this, "Then Zerubbabel the son of Shealtiel and Jeshua the son of Jozadak arose and began to rebuild the house of God which is in Jerusalem; and the prophets of God were with them supporting them." 2 Kings 2:3 has this passage, "Then the sons of the prophets who were at Bethel came out to Elisha and said to him, 'Do you know that the Lord will take away your master [Elijah] from over you today?' And he said, 'Yes, I know; be still!'" And in verse 15, "Now when the sons of the prophets who were at Jericho opposite him saw him, they said, 'The spirit of Elijah rests on Elisha.' And they came to meet him and bowed themselves to the ground before him." In 1 Kings 18:4 we gain some idea of just how many prophets there were, "When Jezebel destroyed the prophets of the Lord, Obadiah took a hundred prophets and hid them by fifties in a cave, and provided them with bread and water."

The name *Essene* is Greek, and though it is and continues to be attributed to the communities at Qumran and Mount Carmel, *none* of the scrolls contain this name and there is no evidence that the communities ever used the name *Essene!*

The origin of the name is difficult to trace, but we do have some information that leads us to the term "Essene." Philo used *Essaioi*, and according to his etymology it signifies "holiness." (*Quod Omnis Probus Liber*, XII. 75–87.) And the Essenes were considered to be a most holy community. In Pliny the Elder's Latin text it is *Esseni.* (*Natural History*, 5:73) And even though the scrolls never used any *singular* name to identify their community, they did refer to themselves by various *descriptive* terms, such as "the Keepers of the Covenant" and "Doers of the Law." Interestingly, "Doers of the Law" in Hebrew is *Osei ha-Torah*, and *Osei* (meaning "to do") is a form of *Osim* (meaning "doers") and is pronounced *oseem*. Thus the "Doers of the Law" may have been called "the Oseem" (phonetically), leading us possibly to "Ossenes"—and in fact, Epiphanius wrote about a Judaic sect called "Ossenes." (*Panarion*, 1:19.) This may have been the Hebrew source for the Greek name *Essenes.*

Even so, there is much confusion and misinformation about these people, and much of it appears to come from the classical historians.

Baigent and Leigh gave many examples of the misunderstanding and confusion over the Essenes. (*The Dead Sea Scrolls Deception*, p. 170) Here are some obvious misunderstandings:

• According to the classical historians, the Essenes were celibate; yet researchers of the Qumran area found the graves of women and children and a scroll titled "Community Rule" which contained regulations governing marriage and the raising of children.

• Strangely, the classical writers that I listed above never mentioned the *solar* calendar used by the Essenes, yet it was profoundly different than the established *lunar* calendar used by the Jews of that time. How could they miss this striking detail?

• Philo wrote that the Essenes did not have animal sacrifice, which was practiced by orthodox Jews at the Temple in those times; yet the Qumran caves contained a scroll called the "Temple Scroll" containing precise instructions for conducting animal sacrifice.

• Josephus declares that Herod the Great honored the Essenes, yet the scrolls indicate otherwise, identifying Herod and his dynasty among their enemies.

- Classical writers identified the Essenes as pacifists, yet among the scrolls at Qumran is a "War Scroll," clearly indicating otherwise. And Qumran was a *fortified* site and the community had a *forge* for making weapons.

Why these differences? Modern researchers believe it is due to various divisions within the greater Essene community, and Edgar Cayce agrees. Even Josephus acknowledges that some Essenes did indeed marry and have children, while others were celibate. (*The Wars of the Jews*, Book II, Chapter 8) Some Essenes may have been pacifists and some zealot warriors. The Scriptures themselves acknowledge the presence of zealots among the population, even among the followers of Jesus.

But the best reason may be that the classical writers never had *access* to the inner community because anyone who wanted to become a member had to endure a *three-year* qualifying period!

There is some indication that segments of the greater Essenes community may have actually maintained relationships with the orthodox Jews at the main temple in Jerusalem and some with the non–Jewish authorities, including Herod the Great. The Essenes may have infiltrated these potentially dangerous groups in order to keep tabs on them and their plans, avoiding any surprising changes that might endanger their community.

Another reason for confusion among the classical historians is that there were many religious communities living in Roman Judea at that time, and despite their differences many were called *Essenes* (meaning something akin to "holy ones"). The Qumran and Mount Carmel communities were placed in the same collective pool with all the others who were ascetic, mystical, and messianic. Josephus numbered the Essenes in the thousands, possibly because of this broad use the term *Essene*, and considered them to be the third major sect of Judaism at that time—the other two being Pharisees and Sadducees: "For there are three philosophical sects among the Jews. The followers of the first of which are the Pharisees; of the second, the Sadducees; and the third sect, which pretends to a severer discipline, are called Essenes. These last are Jews by birth, and seem to have a greater affection for each other than other sects have." (*The Wars of the Jews*, 2:124)

According to Josephus, the Essenes had settled "in large numbers in every town" in Judea. Philo speaks of "more than four thousand" Essaioi living in "Palestine and Syria," (*Quod Omnis Probus Liber*. XII.75) and "in many cities of Judaea and in many villages and grouped in great societies of many members." (*Hypothetica.* 11:1, in Eusebius. *Praeparatio Evangelica,* VIII) [Note: *Palestine* was the Roman name for the region, biblically it was *Canaan.*]

In Edgar Cayce's discourse numbered 254-109, he translated the name Essene to mean something akin to *"expectancy"* in English. And since the Essenes were considered by almost every classical record to be a "messianic" community, Cayce's word choice would seem appropriate. "Expectancy" clearly indicates that they believed in the prophecy of a messiah that was given to Daniel by the archangel Gabriel in chapter 9 of the biblical Book of Daniel (9:25-26). But Cayce explained that there was a bigger vision among these souls. He went on to explain that those who are seekers and "students of spirituality" and the "phases of spiritual evolution" have an *"expectancy* of a new order, of a fulfilling of or a return to those activities that may bring about the time for redemption of the world." This worldview fits as well, because the Essenes had satellite communities as far away as India. (*Manimekalai,* by Merchant Prince Shattan, verse (*gatha*) 27)

Cayce continued explaining that the Essenes felt that the basis of human instruction and direction needed to be not so materialistic and commercial but more spiritual because ultimately human souls are *eternal spiritual beings.* And as such, we are destined to be *celestial* beings who are only *temporarily* incarnating terrestrially. We temporarily live in this physical world as terrestrial beings, and though it is intentional and purposeful, our true nature and destiny is as spirit-souls with higher celestial *minds.*

This Cayce reading goes on to indicate that it is important to enable individuals and groups to *prepare* themselves to be channels through which the more perfect way may be seen and understood. Thus, the need for the "School of the Prophets" as was begun by the high priest Melchizedek, the "King of Salem," who broke bread and drank wine with Abraham (Genesis 14:18), and later by the prophet Samuel (I Samuel 10 and 19) and developed further by the prophet Elijah, ultimately leading to the establishment of the sect of the Essenes and their temple at Mount Carmel. (I Kings 18) Some believe that this temple was initially near the cave in which Elijah heard God's "still, small voice." (I Kings 19:12)

According to Cayce, the initial purpose of the Essenes was individual preparation for *spiritual birth*. Jesus gave this same teaching to Nicodemus when he stated the importance of being born again—physical birth was only half of the whole human journey, one also had to be born of the Spirit. (John 3) This was true because all humans are eternal spirit beings and only temporarily physical ones. A secondary purpose was to prepare enlightened people to go out into the world as light bearers to counterbalance the soul-crushing darkness of selfishness, materialism, and worldliness.

However, Cayce alerts us that the Essenes were not a homogenous group but, like the Christian Protestant faith, had many denominations, many branches of varying beliefs, rules, rituals, and lifestyles. At various times and places these differing branches were called Nazarites, School of the Prophets, Hasidees, Therapeutae, Nazarenes, and even the Great White Brotherhood (though the name may imply males only, Cayce revealed that sisters were members of this brother-sisterhood as well). Some of these denominations even had Gentiles among their membership! You recall how the apostle Peter was shocked when the Holy Spirit descended upon uncircumcised, pork-eating, partying Gentiles! (Acts 10:45) Cayce also taught that the Essenes considered women to be *equals* with men, and even allowed them to serve in temple ceremonies: "This was the beginning of the period where women were considered as equals with the men in their activities, in their abilities to formulate, to live, to be channels."(254-109) Interestingly, there is confirmation of this in the scriptures when the baby Jesus is shown to a female prophet at the temple. (Luke 2:36-38) There is only one temple that would have allowed such a thing to occur, and it had to be the Essene temple on Mount Carmel.

This same discourse of Cayce's states that they "joined [the community] by dedication—usually by their parents. It was a free will thing all the way through, but they were restricted only in the matter of certain foods and certain associations in various periods—which referred to the sex, as well as to the food or drink."

The readings explained that Jesus did not just suddenly appear but was the result of nearly three-hundred years of Essene efforts to *prepare the way* for the coming of the promised Messiah *Spirit* and the Messiah *Consciousness* into the earth! The Essenes had read the scriptures carefully. They knew that God had promised a maiden would conceive and birth a sacred boy that would be known as "God with us" (Isaiah 7:14, *Emmanuel*). And the archangel Gabriel had prophesied the coming of an "Anointed One" to challenge the world in Daniel 9:25–26. Therefore, the Essenes where looking for a special young woman who would be the channel of a light teacher from God.

Cayce was asked to describe the process of selection and the training of those set aside as holy girls and possible mothers for the "Anointed One" (*Messiah* in Hebrew and *Christ* in Greek). He explained that all candidates were first "dedicated" by their parents; then later the individuals needed to make a commitment "through growths as to whether they would be merely channels for general services . . . or special services." At various times the leadership of the Essenes would put out a call for special services. In the case of the birth of the Messiah, twelve young girls were chosen from many who had been dedicated by their parents and then personally committed themselves to a special service. Cayce's readings describe how they were restricted from activities and associations that normal young women enjoyed, especially as relate to the prevailing concepts of what an ideal women was: attractive beauty, sensual, and sexually learned. Such ideas were not a part of the daily training and experiences for these girls. They did not beautify themselves to appeal to men. Rather, they spent their time in spiritually uplifting activities, such as lessons in the true origin and destiny of humanity as souls, lessons and discussions concerning the original creation and the purpose for woman, of divine service as channels of light into this world, of creative, uplifting movement and music that aroused and raised the soul and mind rather than the lusts of the body, lessons and practice with praying and singing, caring for others, doing good in the community, and practicing the "Fruits of the Spirit." (Galatians 5:22) They were very busy girls.

Cayce's reading stated that the life's work of the Essenes, from very early times, "were given to alms, good deeds, missionary activities—as would be termed today." The reading also indicates that many Essene trained individuals, including many women, eventually lived busy lives in the everyday community, even in the households of wealthy and important citizens. Shockingly, a trained Essene woman served in the household of Herod! For example, in Herod's palace his third wife's assistant was a trained member of the Essenes! The reading states: "Through the manner and conduct of life of that individual [the assistant], and the associations and activities, the entity [Herod's third wife] gained knowledge of that group's activities [the Essenes]." The wife sought out a secret meeting with one of the Essene wise men and learned the fundamentals of the faith and daily practice.

Here's a segment of Cayce's discourses on Essene practices and the birth of Jesus:

Please describe the Essene wedding, in temple, of Mary and Joseph, giving the form of ceremony and customs at that time.

(A) This followed very closely the form outlined in Ruth [one of only two biblical books named after a woman, the other being Esther]. It was not in any way a supplanting but a cherishing of the sincerity of purpose in the activities of individuals.

When you read the biblical book of Ruth, you do not find any wedding ceremony; rather, you find an older landowner named Boaz honoring the selflessness of the maiden Ruth in caring for her widowed mother-in-law Naomi. Boaz also honors the customs and rules of his community by allowing a younger suitor who, according to tradition, has first right to marry Ruth and take ownership of Naomi's deceased husband's land. The younger suitor does not accept the offer, so Boaz is free to marry Ruth, whom he cherishes because of her *sincerity of purpose* the Cayce's reading indicates.

Shifting now to Cayce's reading 2067-11, Cayce speaks to how the maid Mary was among the chosen ones to serve as channels of the Messiah and how she was "indicated" on the stairway to the altar of Mount Carmel's temple by "the hovering of the angel." This angel also made the "annunciation" of Mary as the chosen one to her mother Anna and to Judy, the Essene priestess who became one of the main teachers of the young Jesus (we'll learn more about her in a later chapter).

There will be much more on the Essenes and Mary in chapter 6. Here, though, is a fundamental statement by Cayce about this community:

Hence the group we refer to here as the Essenes, which was the out-growth of the periods of preparations from the teachings by Melchizedek, as propagated by Elijah and Elisha and Samuel. These were set aside for preserving themselves in direct line of choice for the offering of themselves as channels through which there might come the new or the divine origin, see?   254-109

Could we have an Essene group today? Could we have a School of the Prophets? We suspect not. First of all, modern society today is generally against cults—even delineations of the faith are beginning to breakdown, moving toward a more ecumenical view of religious diversity. Secondly, given today's attitudes, most people do not dedicate their children to churches or organizations, especially secret ones. Thirdly, there is a worldwide demand for more regulatory oversight of organizations and groups, and more transparency into their internal activities and handling of young people, especially children. And given the world's anxiety with terrorists, sleeper cells, cults, especially of a religious nature, it would be unlikely that such a group could form today without a least some serious "watch-dog" group interference, if not the local or national government agency getting involved.

However, Western beliefs in individual freedom allow people to get into whatever interests they desire, no matter how unusual they are, as long as they do not threaten the fabric of society. Even so, terrorism is cutting into the broader freedoms as governments and groups feel the need to be more aware, prepared, and preemptive.

The wisdom that came through Edgar Cayce consistently guided him and his little band of visionaries to *not* form a cult or schism of any kind. The guidance was to first apply the concepts and practices in their own lives and then present them to others as "see for yourself," sharing the benefits experienced but never attempting to push the information on others or draw others into a cabal. Over these past many years, the A.R.E. has continued to make opportunities available to seekers of better health, greater consciousness, and heightened spirituality, while allowing for as much individual variations as possible without leaving the foundational concepts that came through Cayce's amazing discourses and the faiths they were built upon.

The breadth of topics covered by the readings has made for a diverse organization with a massage and hydrotherapy school, a transpersonal psychology and leadership university, annual conferences on everything from ancient mysteries to modern remote viewing, from energy medicine to intuitive medical analysis, from mystical, universal forms of Judaism and Christianity to the *physics* of God!

The little organization that began with one amazing psychic, Edgar Cayce, has grown into an international association of seekers with diverse cultural, national, educational, and spiritual backgrounds and perspectives—each retaining his or her own *inner* source of revelation and guidance. This open association of seekers allows for much diversity with one overarching and underlying ideal: There is one infinite source of life, and there is an ultimate oneness of *all* souls from and in that one source. Common among these seekers is a belief that eventually evil, violence, hatred, and hierarchical dominance will vanish, leaving only goodness, love, and mutual appreciation for one another.

Chapter 3

Essenes' Scrolls–
Found

Despite a few alternative views, most every researcher agrees that the scrolls found in caves next to the Dead Sea belonged to the community that lived in Qumran, and most researchers agree that this was the community of those now known as the Essenes. However, most of the scrolls were *not written* by the Essenes; many appear to be *collections* of important spiritual and historical documents that may have been written elsewhere by various *other* groups or authors and then collected as well as preserved by the Essene community at Qumran.

Some *forty percent* of the scrolls are *copies* of various texts in the Hebrew Bible, the Tanakh! *Tanakh* is an acronym of the first Hebrew letter of each of the three traditional sections of the Hebrew Bible: *Torah* ("Teaching," the Five Books of Moses), *Nevi'im* ("Prophets") and *Ketuvim* ("Writings")—thus: **TaNaKh** (there are no vowels in Hebrew, so they are added to help with pronunciation).

Roughly *thirty percent* of the scrolls are spiritual documents not included in the Hebrew Bible but are considered to be important, such as the Book of Enoch, the Book of Tobit, Psalms 152-155, the Wisdom of

Sirach, Jubilees, and so on—all of these documents are from the Second Temple Period (516 BCE to 70 CE).

There were two Temple Periods. Nebuchadnezzar II, who was the king of the Babylonian Empire and reigned from roughly 605 to 562 BCE, destroyed the first temple. He was the king who constructed the famous Hanging Gardens of Babylon (one of the Seven Wonders of the Ancient World). In 587 BCE he invaded Jerusalem and destroyed the First Temple of Israel, which had been constructed by the Israelite King Solomon in 957 BCE. The Second Temple of Israel was built after the Persians conquered Babylon. Esther, the famous Jewish queen of the Persian king Ahasuerus, convinced her husband to allow her people to return to Jerusalem and to help them rebuild their temple. The Book of Esther is found in both the Ketuvim of the Jewish Tanakh and the Christian Old Testament. While only a small portion is in the Protestant version, the whole text is in the Catholic version of the Bible. The Second Temple was completed in 516 BCE. However, in 70 CE the Roman general Titus destroyed the Second Temple, which Jesus had prophesied nearly forty years earlier in the Gospel of Matthew, chapter 24, when his disciples were admiring the Second Temple.

The remaining scrolls, roughly thirty percent, cover various activities and rules of the Qumran community. They are: The Copper Scroll, The Community Scroll, The War Scroll, The Temple Scroll, The Damascus Scroll, The Habakkuk Commentary, and so on. Scholars have dated some of these scrolls to as early as 408 BCE and some as late as 73 CE. You recall that in 73 CE nine hundred Jewish zealots held out against a 5000–man Roman legion at Masada (a majestic plateau in the western desert of Judea, south of the Qumran caves along the Dead Sea). Masada marked the end of a significant Jewish presence in Jerusalem, both for the traditional Jews and the burgeoning followers of Jesus Christ, who were Jews that referred to their movement as "The Way." (Acts 24:14) Most of the "Christian" Jews migrated to Asia Minor (modern–day Turkey) and began the now–famous "Seven Churches of Asia Minor" found in the Book of the Revelation: Ephesus, Smyrna, Pergamos (Pergamum), Thyatira, Sardis, Philadelphia, and Laodicea. (Revelation 1:11) These communities became known as *Christian*, but this is merely a Hellenization of *Messianic*, which they also called themselves. It is the same as the Greek *Khristos* (Anglicized as Christ), which was simply a translation of the Hebrew *Moshiach* (modern *Mashiach*), both words meaning "Anointed One" in their respective languages. The term comes from Exodus 30:25–30 where the holy anointing oil was used to sanctify one for a special spiritual purpose.

The Dead Sea Scrolls were initially discovered by Bedouin shepherds Muhammed Edh-Dhib, Jum'a Muhammed, and Khalil Musa between November 1946 and February 1947. The shepherds discovered seven scrolls housed in jars in a cave at the Qumran site. Dr. John Trever of the American Schools of Oriental Research (ASOR) later reconstructed the story of the scrolls from several interviews with the shepherds. Jum'a Muhammed noticed the caves but Muhammed Edh-Dhib was the first to actually fall into one of these caves. He found some scrolls, which Dr. Trever identified as the Isaiah Scroll, Habakkuk Commentary, and the Community Rule. Muhammed Edh-Dhib took them back to the camp to show to his family. The Bedouin eventually took the scrolls to a dealer named Ibrahim 'Ijha in Bethlehem. But after being warned that the scrolls might have been stolen from a synagogue, 'Ijha returned them. An Arab elder suggested that they take the scrolls to Khalil Eskander Shahin, known as "Kando," who was a part-time antiques dealer. The Bedouin left one scroll with Kando and sold three of the scrolls to a Syrian Christian dealer. It was in 1947 that the original seven scrolls caught the attention of Dr. John Trever, who compared the script in the scrolls to that of The Nash Papyrus, the oldest biblical manuscript then known!

As so often happens, war stopped the research. In March of 1948 the Arab-Israeli War forced the scrolls to be moved out of Israel to Beirut. In April 1948, Millar Burrows, head of the ASOR, announced the discovery of the scrolls in a major press release. Later that year, Bishop Mar Samuel, Archbishop of the Syriac Orthodox Church of Antioch, bought the Isaiah Scroll, the Community Rule, the Habakkuk Peshar, and the Genesis Apocryphon. Bishop Samuel showed the scrolls to Professor Ovid R. Sellers, the new Director of ASOR. Professor Sellers attempted to get the Syrians to assist in the search for the cave, but he was unable to pay their price. In early 1948, the government of Jordan gave permission to the Arab Legion to search the area for the Qumran caves. As a result of this, Cave 1 was rediscovered in January 1949 by Belgian United Nations observer Captain Phillipe Lippens and Arab Legion Captain Akkash el-Zebn.

The rediscovery of what became known as "Cave 1" prompted an excavation of the site from February 15 to March 5, 1949 by the Jordanian Department of Antiquities led by British archaeologist and Director of the Jordanian Department of Antiquities, Gerald Lankester Harding, and by Roman Catholic priest Father Roland de Vaux. The Cave 1 site yielded discoveries of additional Dead Sea Scroll fragments, linen cloth, jars, and other artifacts.

In November 1951, Father Roland de Vaux and his team from the ASOR began a full excavation of Qumran. By February 1952, the Bedouin people had discovered thirty fragments in what was to be designated Cave 2. The discovery of a second cave eventually yielded three hundred fragments from thirty-three manuscripts, including fragments of Jubilees, the Wisdom of Sirach, and Ben Sira written in Hebrew (Ben Sira was a second century BCE Jewish scribe and sage in Jerusalem). The following month, March 1952, the ASOR team discovered a third cave! This one had fragments of Jubilees and the now famous Copper Scroll. Between September and December 1952, the fragments and scrolls in Caves 4, 5, and 6 were discovered! Between 1953 and 1956, Father Roland de Vaux led four more archaeological expeditions in the area to uncover scrolls and artifacts. The last cave, Cave 11, was discovered in 1956 and yielded the last fragments to be found in the vicinity of Qumran.

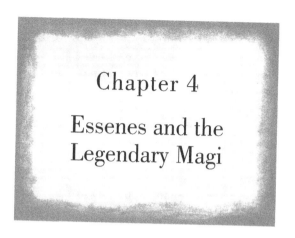

Chapter 4

Essenes and the Legendary Magi

Since the 500s BCE the term "Magi" signified a follower of Zoroaster, the Persian prophet who founded the religion called Zoroastrianism. He was originally known as Zarathustra (660–583 BCE) and the primary sacred text was and remains the *Avesta*, a word that may best correspond with the English word "Praise." It's often referred to as the *Zend-Avesta*, where *Zend* or *Zand* means "interpretation of," thus, the name of the text may be "Interpreted–Praise." There are two forms of manuscripts composing the whole Avesta or Zoroastrian Bible. One is the *Zend-i-Avesta*, in which the individual books are gathered together with their interpretation and commentary. The other manuscript is the *Vendidād Sadeh*, in which the *Yasna* (ritual), *Visperad* (festival recitations), and *Vendidād* (the laws or rules) are set in order and used in the ceremonies. The aim of a Zoroastrian ceremony is to preserve the integrity of the cosmic good of God's creation—a tall order!

Zarathustra experienced a vision in which the "Wise Lord" or "God of Light" (*Ahura Mazda*) instructed him to learn, to live, and to teach specific concepts, ideals, and practices to the people. Fundamentally, the teaching is that the "bountiful mind and spirit" (*spenta mainyu*, where "mainyu" means both *mind* and *spirit,* and "spenta" means *bounteous)* is in a constant struggle with the "destructive mind and spirit" (*angra mainyu,* where "angora" means *destructive, inhibitive, malign,* and the like). Since human beings have been given the freewill power to live as their hearts move them, they must choose between these two states of being and thinking, and they will grow to personify one or the other of these dual states of being—and thereby becoming more *constructive* or more *destructive.* The former leads one to be more selfless and caring as well as a light and comfort to all, while the latter leads one to the point of being totally self–centered and selfish, *taking* life rather than *giving* life. See Deuteronomy 30:15 for the Hebrew version of this freewill gift in which the same options are set before us: good and evil, light and dark. Eventually the time of the opportunity to choose freely will come to a close and the Bountiful Mind and Spirit will dissolve the destructive mind and spirit, while all those who chose the constructive life will rejoice in their eternal life with the Bountiful Mind and Spirit, which was their original Creator. These two opposing forces are often spoken of and even personified in the Avesta texts as Light and Darkness, Good and Evil.

Zoroastrians hold these three principles to be their pillars of wisdom: "Good thoughts, good words, good deeds" (Avesta, *Vendidād* 21: "Humata, Hūkhta, hvarshta"). Here is another example of their fundamental principles:

Question: By what means can one make Bountiful Mind and Spirit, His Bountiful Immortals, and the fragrant and pleasant Heaven his own?

Answer: By Wisdom, Contentment, Truthfulness, Gratefulness, Devotedness, Generosity, Moderation, Endeavor, and Trust (in God). By these means, one reaches Heaven and is in sight of God. (Avesta: *Mino-ī-Kherad,* 43:1-14)

You can see how these principles easily fit with Judeo–Christian principles. Consider as an example the writings of the Christian disciple Paul who also saw two forces struggling against one another, the spirit and the flesh, and listed the "fruits" of these:

I say, walk by the Spirit, and you won't fulfill the lust of the flesh. For the flesh lusts against the Spirit and the Spirit against the flesh; and these are contrary to one other, that you may not do the things that you desire. But if you are led by the Spirit, you are not under the law. Now the works of the flesh are obvious, which are: adultery, sexual immorality, uncleanness, lustfulness, idolatry, sorcery, hatred, strife, jealousies, outbursts of anger, rivalries, divisions, heresies, envyings, murders, drunkenness, orgies, and things like these; of which I forewarn you, even as I also forewarned you, that those who practice such things will not inherit the Kingdom of God. But the fruit of the Spirit is love, joy, peace, patience, kindness, goodness, faithfulness, gentleness, and self-control. Against such things there is no law. Those who belong to Christ have crucified the flesh with its passions and lusts. If we live by the Spirit, let's also walk by the Spirit. Let's not become conceited, provoking one another, and envying one another. (Galatians 5:17-26)

Edgar Cayce's discourses saw the struggle to be between love and selfishness, seeing God as the spirit of love, and selfishness as misuse of the gift of free will for self-gratification, and self-exaltation: "The only sin is self . . . " He saw this as the reasoning behind the two great commandments: love God and love one another.

In addition to these examples, some of the Zoroastrian stories are also found in the stories of the Jews and Christians. For example, Zoroaster, like Jesus, is tempted by the personification of the Destructive Mind and Spirit, or Satan in the Christian story, to follow its ways with the promise that Zoroaster would become the sovereign of the whole world! But Zoroaster, also like Jesus, rejects the Destructive Mind and Spirit's temptation, pushing it out of his personal mind and spirit. (Vendidad 19 and Matthew 4:1-12).

Where did Zoroastrianism and its Magi first connect with the Jews and thereby the Jewish sect of the Essenes? It can be traced all the way back to the Babylonian captivity of the Jews of the First Temple, when the First Temple was destroyed and the Jewish captives were carried off to Babylon by Nebuchadnezzar II (597-582 BCE)—even the prophet Daniel was among the captives. At this same time and after, Zoroastrianism was the religion of Persia (modern-day Iran) and Babylon was their next-door neighbor (a portion of modern-day Iraq). When the Persians finally invaded and conquered Babylon (539 BCE), they eventually liberated the captive Jews. But by the time they were allowed to return to Jerusalem, these Jews would have heard and recorded the religious beliefs of their liberators and perhaps possessed copies of the Zend-Avesta. They would have taken some of these wonderful ideas and texts back with them, and these would have become some of the documents of the Second Temple period that made their way into the caves in Qumran.

Where does Zoroastrianism connect with early Christianity? Many of the Essenes considered themselves to be "Messianic," preparing for the birth of the Messiah, and many of them considered Jesus to be that Messiah. They, therefore, became followers of "The Way" of Jesus' teachings, still considering themselves to be Jews, but "Jews of The Way." What helped them believe that Jesus was the prophesied Messiah? The answer is the legendary Magi coming from the East to honor the birth of Jesus as the "King of the Jews," claiming that the stars indicated this! Some of the Magi were known to be sacred Zoroastrian priests trained in astrology as well as other esoteric wisdom and practices. They even lent their name to the word "magic." In the Gospel of Matthew, 2:1-2, they are called "wise men from the east," but many of the early church leaders referred to them as "magicians." (Drum, W.; 1910; "Magi," *The Catholic Encyclopedia*, New York: Robert Appleton Company) These Magi were of such an enlightened consciousness that they, too, had a dream from God in which God instructed them not to return to King Herod, but to travel a different way back to their country. (Matthew 2:12) And they obeyed the instruction. Herod, angry that he had lost the confidence of the Magi and their knowledge of which newly born male child was to become the "King of the Jews," chose to kill every baby boy two years of age and under—a horrific act that caused the spirit of Rachel to weep inconsolably for her children. (Matthew 2:18) But Joseph and Mary had already fled to Egypt with the baby Jesus, obeying the instruction of an angel in a dream instructing Joseph to flee with the mother and child. (Matthew 2:1-15)

In his masterpiece, *The Histories* (i. 131 et seq.), Herodotus, considered to be the "Father of History," recorded that the Persians from the earliest times considered the sun, moon, stars, earth, the waters, and the wind to be sacred, and everyone should cooperate with them and never abuse, misuse, or contaminate them. Herodotus recorded that the Magi believed in the *propitiation* of the powers of evil (ib. iii. 35, vii. 114), which is considered today to be a basic Christian concept! In other words, through new actions old sins are absolved, as the apostle Peter noted in his epistle: "Above all things being fervent in your love among yourselves; *for love covers a multitude of sins.*" (I Peter 4:8, my italics) Herodotus also wrote that Zoroaster strongly spoke and wrote against demoniacal rites and practices that continued to be practiced. Herodotus described how Zoroastrian priests conducted magical ceremonies to evoke the power and presence of the Bountiful Spirit and Mind, corresponding closely to the Christian practice of evoking the presence and power of the Holy Spirit—which was for a time conducted in secret so as not to be labeled divination by the Inquisitor. Even Nostradamus recorded how he used a method for evoking the divine presence to generate his visions, writing that he was "seated alone in secret study . . . fear arising and trembling . . . for in divine splendor a god sits nearby." (Century 1, clips from Quatrains 1 and 2) Nostradamus had to cloak his writings in obscure language in order to avoid the wrath of the Inquisitor, especially since Nostradamus' parents were Jews who converted to Catholicism, making them suspect of being under Satan's influence.

As in Kabbalah and Christianity, the Magi had legends and lore of angels as well as heavenly beings akin to *archangels*, called "Immortal Holy Ones" (*Amesha Spentas*). These archangels personified virtues and ideals: Good Mind, Perfect Righteousness, the "wished-for" Kingdom, Harmony, Health, Salvation, and Immortality (or Eternal Life with God).

The Zoroastrians also had the concept of an *incarnation* of God's Light! They called it the "incarnation of light and truth," known as *Mithra* (not to be confused with Roman *Mithraism*). Mithra is derived from *-tra*, meaning "causing to," and *mi-*, meaning "to bind," thus Mithra is he who "causes one to hold to" the covenant, the oath. This is where the Essenes, who referred to themselves as "the Keepers of the Covenant," met with the ancient Mithra and his mission of "binding to the covenant."

Amazingly, Mithra has many titles similar to Jesus (John 14:6), Mithra is called "the Truth," "the Way," "the Light," and more. (Avesta: *Yasna* 1–3) In Old Persian Mithra is called *Mica* and is often connected with *Baga*, the Old Persian word for God; thus *Mica-Baga*, indicates that Mithra was as the Gospel writer John described the Logos, *an incarnation of God*: "In the beginning was the Word (Greek: *Logos*), and the Logos was with God and the Logos was God . . . and all things were created through this One." (John 1:1–3) John later wrote that the Logos became flesh and dwelt among us (John 1:14). Curiously, Mica/Mithra was also described as being an incarnation of the Light, the Truth (found on the *Elamite* tablets of Darius' time).

Here's a Zoroastrian passage from the *Khorda Avesta* (known as the "Little Avesta" and the "Book of Common Prayer"), referring to Mithra as follows:

Whose word is true, who is of the assembly, Who has a thousand ears, the well-shaped one, Who has ten thousand eyes, the exalted one, Who has wide knowledge, the helpful one, Who sleeps not, the ever wakeful. We sacrifice to Mithra, The lord of all countries, Whom the Creator *(Ahura Mazda)* created the most glorious, Of the supernatural, venerable, divine beings. So may there come to us for aid, Both Mithra and the Creator (Ahura), the two exalted ones . . . [Khorda Avesta: *Khwarshed Niyayesh* 5-7; based on an edition by Karl F. Geldner: *Avesta, The Sacred Books of the Parsis;* Stuttgart, 1896; and my edited version of the 2002 digital edition by Joseph H. Peterson, which can be found at: avesta.org/ka/niyayesh.htm]

In the 200s CE, Manicheans wrote that Mithra was an original Savior who rescued "First Man" from the Darkness into which he had plunged. (Widengren, Geo *Mesopotamian* elements in *Manichaeism* (King and Saviour II): *Studies in Manichaean, Mandaean, and Syrian-gnostic religion*, Lundequistska bokhandeln, 1946, p. 10) The disciple Paul refers to a "First Adam" and a "Last Adam": "The first man Adam became a living soul. The last Adam became a life–giving spirit." (I Corinthians 15:45) Christian saint Augustine was once a Manichean but converted to Christianity when the Roman Emperor Theodosius I issued a decree of death for Manichaeans in 382 CE and shortly before the emperor declared Christianity to be the only legitimate religion for the Roman Empire in 391. (Foltz, Richard, *Religions of the Silk Road;* Palgrave Macmillan, 2nd edition, 2010, p. 71)

As in Judaism and Christianity, Zoroastrianism also has the concept of a prophesied Messiah–Savior who will come to make all things right. It is *Saoshyant* (pronounced *soush-yant*), literally meaning "one who brings benefit" and is often referred to as "The Beneficent One." Saoshyant is considered to be the *final* savior of the world. (Avesta: *Farvardin Yast*

13:129) Jesus also spoke of such a final world-ending, heavenly being, but not so much as a benefactor as a gatherer of those who have used free will well:

The lightning comes from the east and shines as far as the west, so will be the coming of the Son of man . . . Immediately after the tribulation of those days the sun will be darkened, and the moon will not give its light, and the stars will fall from heaven, and the powers of the heavens will be shaken; then will appear the sign of the Son of man in heaven, and then all the tribes of the earth will mourn, and they will see the Son of man coming on the clouds of heaven with power and great glory; and he will send out his angels with a loud trumpet call, and they will gather his elect from the four winds, from one end of heaven to the other. (Matthew 24:27-31)

As an aside here, let me share that the ancient Egyptians also had the concept and legend of a Messiah, and it was an immaculately con-ceived Messiah too, as in Mary and Jesus. In the Egyptian legend Isis immaculately conceives Horus, who overthrows the evil Set, who, out the same motivations as Cain, killed his brother Osiris, as Cain killed Abel. Eventually Set's evil is overcome as Horus reigns in wisdom and goodness. Speaking of immaculate conceptions, there is a legend that Zoroaster's mother, *Dughdova*, was a virgin when she conceived Zoro-aster by a shaft of light from Heaven. Even Mithra was born of a virgin and on December 25th! Throughout the legends of world religions and theologies there are tales of virgin births. In Judaism, Sarah was in her nineties and had long ago experienced menopause (the cessation of a woman's biological reproductive ability), yet she conceive, gestated, and birth the Lord-promised Isaac. Virgin births can be found most everywhere: Buddha was born of the virgin Maya after the Holy Ghost descended upon her; in Phrygia, Attis was born of the virgin Nama; the Roman savior Quirrnus was born of a virgin; in Tibet, Indra was born of a virgin; the Greek deity Adonis was born of the virgin Myrrha; in India, the god Krishna was born of the virgin Devaki; even Alexander the Great of Greece was supposedly born of a virgin mother. The idea that heavenly forces can affect earthly, physical outcomes is a concept found throughout spiritual literature. In Genesis chapter 6 we find that the celestial Sons of God could actually conceive physical babies with human women! These babies became known as the Nephilim, legendary giants.

Let's get back to prophecies of coming or returning prophets and messiahs. In Judaism we also find prophets and prophesied prophets to come: "I will raise up for them a prophet like you [the Lord is speaking to Moses] from among their brethren; and I will put my words in his mouth, and he shall speak to them all that I command him." (Deuteronomy 18:18) And later in the book of Daniel: "I saw in the night visions, and behold, with the clouds of heaven there came one like a son of man, and he came to the Ancient of Days and was presented before him. And to him was given dominion and glory and kingdom, that all peoples, nations, and languages should serve him; his dominion is an everlasting dominion, which shall not pass away, and his kingdom one that shall not be destroyed." (Daniel 7:13–14) And in Malachi 4:5–6: "Behold, I will send you Elijah the prophet before the coming of the great and dreadful day of the Lord; And he shall turn the heart of the fathers to the children, and the heart of the children to their fathers, lest I come and smite the earth with a curse." And in Matthew 17:10–13: "Jesus answered and said unto them, Elijah truly shall first come, and restore all things. But I say unto you, That Elijah is come already, and they knew him not, but have done unto him whatsoever they listed. Likewise shall also the Son of man suffer of them. Then the disciples understood that he spoke to them of John the Baptist."

We also find this passage in the Jewish Bible or Christian Old Testament: "Behold, a young woman shall conceive and bear a son, and shall call his name Imman'u-el," which means "God is with us" (Isaiah 7:14), which was later Romanized as *Emmanuel*. In the New Testament we find: "All this happened to fulfill what had been declared by the Lord through the prophet, who said, 'Look, the virgin will become pregnant and will give birth to a son, and they will give him the name Immanuel'—which is translated, 'God with us.'" (Matthew 1:22–23)

Jesus is the fulfillment of this prophecy in Isaiah but then in the twenty-fourth chapter of the Gospel of Matthew, Jesus gives the prophecy of the worldwide coming of the "Son of man" on the clouds of heaven with power and great glory, quoted earlier. Many of these prophecies appear to have two types of messianic occurrences: one is an incarnation of the Light of God that teaches and guides humanity but the other is a final, world-ending coming of a heavenly being that removes all darkness, evil, and temptation, and all return to the original light and love of the Creator or Creative Energies.

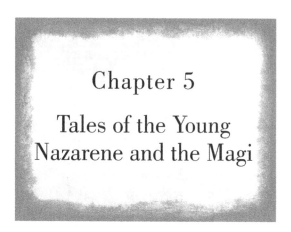

Chapter 5

Tales of the Young
Nazarene and the Magi

B eyond the Gospels there are few historical documents that provide evidence and detail of Jesus' existence. The most famous
and widely accepted as *authentic* comes from the writings of
the historian Flavius Josephus (37 to 100 CE) who wrote the following
description of Jesus in his *Antiquities of the Jews*, Book 18, chapter 3:

Now there was about this time Jesus, a wise man, if it be lawful to call
him a man; for he was a doer of wonderful works, a teacher of such men as
receive the truth with pleasure. He drew over to him both many of the Jews
and many of the Gentiles. He was Christ. And when Pilate, at the suggestion
of the principal men amongst us, had condemned him to the cross, those
that loved him at the first did not forsake him; for he appeared to them alive
again the third day, as the divine prophets had foretold these and ten thousand other wonderful things concerning him. And the tribe of Christians, so
named from him, is not extinct at this day.

In Book 20, chapter 200, Josephus wrote about the stoning of Jesus'
brother in 62 CE, including this line that clearly indicates the existence

of both Jesus and his brother: "James, the brother of Jesus, who was called Christ . . . " See the publication *James the Brother of Jesus: The Key to Unlocking the Secrets of Early Christianity and the Dead Sea Scrolls* by American archaeologist and Biblical scholar Robert H. Eisenman, (Penguin, 1998). It's worth noting that even the Gospels indicate that Jesus had brothers: "While he (Jesus) was still speaking to the people, behold, his mother and his brothers stood outside, asking to speak to him." (Matthew 12:46) And according to the Edgar Cayce readings, Jesus had two brothers, James and Jude, explaining that after Jesus left the family home to travel, Mary and Joseph had more children, as was the custom in those days: "(Q) Did Mary and Joseph have any other children? (A) James, Jude, and the daughter [Ruth]." (5749-7)

There are more of these non-biblical sources, but they have limited scholarly support for their authenticity. One is a letter that appears to have been written by Pontius Pilate to Caesar. In this letter Pilate describes Jesus: "His golden-colored hair and beard gave to his appearance a celestial aspect. He appeared to be about thirty years of age. Never have I seen a sweeter or more serene countenance." I can't image Pilate writing "celestial" and "sweet" as a description of one of his defendants unless he, Pilate, was indeed a sympathizer with Jesus and his message, as some texts do suggest, and his wife, Claudia Procula, had a frightening dream warning not to harm Jesus. (Matthew 27:19) The early Christian scholar Origen of Alexandria suggested in his "Homilies on Matthew" that Claudia Procula had become a secret follower of Jesus Christ.

Another description comes from a Roman official in Judea at the time of Jesus named Lucius Lentulus, ca. 30 CE. It appears in a Latin manuscript, MS 22, in the library of the University of Chicago. The manuscript appears to have been written in Europe, probably Italy, between 1466-1469. In some other medieval manuscripts, the letter is described as being from "Publius Lentulus, Governor of Judea, to the Roman Senate." Since there is no record of a governor of Palestine called Lentulus, the letter is suspect. There was, however, a Publius Cornelius Lentulus (both a father and a son) mentioned by Cicero, who lived in the first century *before* Christ. There was also a Lucius Lentulus who held the office of consul in Rome, not Judea. Perhaps the letter is from this Lentulus, while he was visiting Judea. While we will never know for sure, here's what the letter says:

There lives at this time in Judea a man of singular virtue whose name is Jesus Christ, whom the barbarians esteem as a prophet, but his followers love and adore him as the offspring of the immortal God. He calls back the dead from the graves and heals all sorts of diseases with a word or touch. He is a tall man, well-shaped, and of an amiable and reverend aspect; his hair of a color that can hardly be matched, falling into graceful curls, waving about and very agreeable crouching upon his shoulders, parted on the crown of the head, running as a stream to the front after fashion of the Nazarites. His forehead high, large and imposing; his cheeks without spot or wrinkle, beautiful with a lovely red; his nose and mouth formed with exquisite symmetry; his beard, and of a color suitable to his hair, reaching below his chin and parted in the middle like a fork; his eyes bright blue, clear and serene. Look innocent, dignified, manly and mature. In proportion of body most perfect, and captivating; his arms and hands delectable to behold. He rebukes with majesty, councils with mildness. His whole address whether in word or deed, being eloquent and grave. No man has seen him laugh, yet his manners are exceedingly pleasant, but he has wept frequently in the presence of men. He is temperate, modest and wise. A man for his extraordinary beauty and perfection, surpassing the children of men in every sense.

Of solid authenticity are documents from later periods, long after Jesus' incarnation, giving evidence to his life and influence. For example, Roman historian Tacitus wrote in 110 CE his account of the persecution of Christians under the emperor Nero, which occurred at the same time as the burning of Rome in 64 CE. Nero blamed the burning on the Christians, who were already hated by the Romans. Tacitus wrote: "Their name is derived from *Christ*, whom the procurator Pontius Pilate had executed in the reign of Tiberius." Tacitus explained that the "pernicious superstition" to which Christ had given rise to in Judea had spread far and wide, even to Rome. Tacitus never uses the name "Jesus," only "Christ," when referring to the founder of the faith. We know that very early the followers of Jesus began referring to him by the Greek word for messiah, "christos," meaning the same as the Hebrew word *mashiach* (first used in Daniel 9:25–26 by the archangel Gabriel), which is transliterated to *messiah*. As we have already seen, the word literally means "anointed one." Tacitus' writings give support to the existence and ultimate sentence, crucifixion, of an individual in Palestine known as *Christ*, who began a movement that gained widespread influence some eighty years after his execution.

A letter, written in 111 CE, by Pliny the Younger, the governor of Asia Minor (modern Turkey), asks Emperor Trajan (97–117 CE) how Pliny should deal with Christians. It describes the Christians as adherents to a superstition who sing hymns to Christ "as to a god."

In a biography of Emperor Claudius (41–54 CE), Roman historian Suetonius wrote that in 49 CE the emperor "expelled the Jews from Rome, who had on the instigation of Chrestus continually caused disturbances." These disturbances may have been due to the Jews in Rome becoming either angered or inspired by a Christian agitator named Chrestus. Or Chrestus may also be a Latin variation of the name Christ. Emperor Claudius' expulsion of the Jews from Rome is actually mentioned in the Bible in Acts 18:2.

In the Talmud, a handbook of Jewish law, lore, and teachings, Jesus (*Yeshu* in Hebrew) is described as being born the illegitimate son of a Roman soldier called Panther, and that he practiced magic, ridiculed the wise, seduced and stirred up the people, gathered five disciples about him, and was hanged on the eve of the Passover (in those days *hanged* meant *crucified*, as in "hanged on a cross").

The most detailed information of Jesus comes from the biblical testaments: the Gospels, the Epistles, and the Revelation. In addition to these, there are many other Christian manuscripts and documents beyond the New Testament.

The activities surrounding Jesus' birth, though initially only known to a few within the family's inner circle, were profound, indicating a rare incarnation was about to happen. Jesus' mother, Mary, was visited by the angel Gabriel, who informed her of what was about to happen to her, and the angel's promise was confirmed when Mary came into the presence of her cousin Elizabeth, who was already pregnant with John the Baptist. Here are the passages:

The angel Gabriel was sent from God to a city of Galilee, named Nazareth, to a virgin pledged to be married to a man whose name was Joseph, of the house of David. The virgin's name was Mary. Having come in, the angel said to her, "Rejoice, you highly favored one! The Lord is with you. Blessed are you among women!" But when she saw him, she was greatly troubled at the saying, and considered what kind of salutation this might be. The angel said to her, "Don't be afraid, Mary, for you have found favor with God. Behold, you will conceive in your womb, and bring forth a son, and will call his name "Jesus." He will be great, and will be called the Son of the Most High. The Lord God will give him the throne of his father, David, and he will reign over the house of Jacob forever. There will be no end to his kingdom." Mary said to the angel, "How can this be, seeing I am a virgin?" The angel answered her, "The Holy Spirit will come upon you, and the power of the Most High will overshadow you. Therefore also the holy one who is born from you will be called the Son of God. Behold, Elizabeth, your relative, also has conceived a son in her old age; and this is the sixth month with her who was called barren. For everything spoken by God is possible." Mary said, "Behold, the handmaid of the Lord; be it to me according to your word." The angel departed from her. Mary arose in those days and went into the hill country with haste, into a city of Judah, and entered into the house of Zacharias and greeted Elizabeth. It happened, when Elizabeth heard Mary's greeting, that the baby leaped in her womb, and Elizabeth was filled with the Holy Spirit. She called out with a loud voice, and said, "Blessed are you among women, and blessed is the fruit of your womb! Why am I so favored, that the mother of my Lord should come to me? For behold, when the voice of your greeting came into my ears, the baby leaped in my womb for joy! Blessed is she who believed, for there will be a fulfillment of the things which have been spoken to her from the Lord!" Mary said, "My soul magnifies the Lord. My spirit has rejoiced in God my Savior, for he has looked at the humble state of his hand-maid. For behold, from now on, all generations will call me blessed. For he who is mighty has done great things for me. Holy is his name. His mercy is for generations of generations on those who fear him. He has shown strength with his arm. He has scattered the proud in the imagination of their heart. He has put down princes from their thrones; and has exalted the lowly. He has filled the hungry with good things. He has sent the rich away empty. He has given help to Israel, his servant, that he might remember mercy, as he spoke to our fathers, to Abraham and his seed forever." (Luke 1:26-55)

Joseph, Jesus' earthly father, also received a message from an angel that conveyed the specialness of this coming child. Here are those passages:

After his mother, Mary, was engaged to Joseph, before they came together, she was found pregnant by the Holy Spirit. Joseph, her husband, being a righteous man, and not willing to make her a public example, intended to put her away secretly. But when he thought about these things, behold, an angel of the Lord appeared to him in a dream, saying, "Joseph, son of David, don't be afraid to take to yourself Mary, your wife, for that which is conceived in her is of the Holy Spirit. She shall bring forth a son. You shall call his name Jesus, for it is he who shall save his people from their sins." Now all this has happened, that it might be fulfilled which was spoken by the Lord through the prophet [Isaiah], saying, "Behold, the virgin shall be with child, And shall bring forth a son. They shall call his name Emmanuel; Which is, being interpreted, "'God with us.'" Joseph arose from his sleep, and did as the angel of the Lord commanded him. (Matthew 1:20-24)

As mentioned earlier, the Revelation identifies Jesus as "the root and the offspring of David" (Revelation 22–16). He is even referred to as "Son of David" (Mark 10:48). The Gospels attempt to show that this linkage is not simply esoteric but physical. Matthew's Gospel opens this way: "The book of the Genealogy of Jesus Christ, the son of David, the son of Abraham," and then proceeds to trace the lineage of Joseph, Jesus' earthly father, back through David to Abraham. In Luke's Gospel, 3:23–38, we also find Jesus' genealogy, but this one traces it all the way back through David and Abraham to Adam.

Another connection is that Jesus' parents were of the city of Bethlehem, which was David's hometown. This is why Mary and Joseph had to leave their residence in the town of Nazareth, in the hills of Galilee, to journey back to Bethlehem to register for the taxation. The emperor had ordered all to return to their place of origin to register. Bethlehem was the Davidic family's place of origin. As the Gospels tell the story, while Joseph and Mary were in Bethlehem, Jesus was born, thus making his birthplace another tie-in with David.

Though the Gospels tell us that his birth was modest, it was not without fanfare and notice. Three Magi (plural of Latin *magus*; Greek *magoi*, meaning "magician," perhaps referring to their ability to read the stars) journeyed from the East looking for a prophesied child, born at this specific time and location. Psalm 71:10 may have actually prophesied the coming of the Magi and given a description of them: "The kings of Tarshish [also Tharsis; a Sanskrit word meaning "sea coast"] and the islands shall offer presents; the kings of the Arabians and of Saba [modern-day Yemen, then a wealthy trading location] shall bring him gifts; and all the kings of the earth shall adore him." Historically, these Magi are believed to have been a remnant of an outlawed priestly caste of the Pre-Persian Medes. The original lands of the Medes were estimated to have been from the Caspian Sea to India, engulfing modern Turkey, Iraq, Armenia, and Persia. When Darius became king of Persia in 521 BCE, this priestly caste was outlawed, though secretly their guidance continued to be sought by the Persian leaders for hundreds of years. This means that the modern Christian belief that the Magi were kings is not supported by the historical record, though they were "kingly," meaning rich and accompanied by an entourage that would have attracted much attention and wonder. They were either brought before the king of Judea, Herod the Great, concerning the reason for their presence in his country or wisely requested an audience with him before he commanded it. As we know, once Herod heard of their reason for coming, he ordered the death of all male children under the age of two in an attempt to kill the prophesied "King of the Jews."

Herod's order to kill all male babies less than two years of age forced the Holy Family to flee to Egypt for safety. Luke's Gospel contradicts Matthew's, having the family first return to Nazareth after the birth (Luke 2:39), rather than immediately fleeing directly from Bethlehem to Egypt, as Matthew tells it (Matt. 2:13–14). The family would not have been in Egypt long because Herod the Great died in 4 CE, and his kingdom was divided among his sons by the Roman emperor. His son Herod Antipas became the regional ruler of Galilee, which included the town of Nazareth, Jesus' childhood home from about five years of age. The Bible records that Jesus' earthly father, Joseph, received in a dream the message that he could take his child back into the lands of Israel because those who had sought his death were dead (Matthew 2:19–20).

In Nazareth, Jesus would have been raised to study the Torah, obey the Law, pray, and attend the synagogue. He and his family would have made pilgrimages to the Temple in Jerusalem, as was customary. In fact, in Luke we are told that Jesus and his family went to the Jerusalem Temple every year at Passover. Luke records it this way in 2:40–52:

The child was growing, and was becoming strong in spirit, being filled with wisdom, and the grace of God was upon him. His parents went every year to Jerusalem at the feast of the Passover. When he was twelve years old, they went up to Jerusalem according to the custom of the feast, and when they had fulfilled the days, as they were returning, the boy Jesus stayed behind in Jerusalem. Joseph and his mother didn't know it; supposing him to be in the company, they went a day's journey, and they looked for him among their relatives and acquaintances. When they didn't find him, they returned to Jerusalem, looking for him. It happened after three days they found him in the Temple, sitting in the midst of the teachers, both listening to them and asking them questions. All who heard him were amazed at his understanding and his answers. When they saw him, they were astonished, and his mother said to him, "Son, why have you treated us this way? Behold, your father and I were anxiously looking for you." He said to them, "Why were you looking for me? Didn't you know that I must be in my Father's house?" They didn't understand the saying which he spoke to them. And he went down with them, and came to Nazareth. He was subject to them, and his mother kept all these sayings in her heart. And Jesus increased in wisdom and stature, and in favor with God and men.

Return of the Magi

According to Edgar Cayce's reading of the Akashic record, the Magi returned several times to Galilee to visit the Holy Family and keep up with the progress of the boy's growth. They returned at least five times, and not always the same Magi. Cayce says, "They came from Persia, India, Egypt [initially], and also from Chaldea, Gobi, and what is now the Indo or Tao land." According to these readings, at the fifth visit, when Jesus had become "of age" (which in those days would have been twelve years old), the Magi took him from Jerusalem to their temples for training and testing. These temples were in Persia (modern–day Iran), India, and Egypt. (2067-7)

Cayce explained that the three Wise Men, as they are also called, and their gifts "represent in the metaphysical sense the three phases of man's experience in materiality: gold, the material; frankincense, the ether or ethereal; myrrh, the healing force as brought with same; or body, mind, soul." In these readings, Egypt was the source for the gold.

But in two different readings Cayce gives the source of the incense to Persia in one (1908-1, a Persian Wise Man named *Achlar*) and to India in another (256-1, an Indian Wise Man named *Ashtueil*). Perhaps, in one of the many visits, the Wise Man from Persia brought the frankincense, while in another visit, the one from India brought it. In those days, myrrh came from east India. Myrrh was used in the holy oil of the Jews and the *Kyphi* of the Egyptians. In the initial visitation by the Magi, it is likely that the myrrh came from India, the frankincense from Persia, and the gold from Egypt. Therefore, using Cayce's correlations, we could conclude that ancient Egypt represented the material phase, ancient Persia the ethereal phase, and ancient India the healing phase of human experience.

As to the young Jesus' training and testing, the readings say that he first went to Persia. There he would have been trained and tested according to the ways of Zoroastrianism, from the sacred texts Avesta and the *Gathas* ("Older Hymns"). This faith is at the same time monotheistic and dualistic: teaching that there is only one God but two distinct forces battling for the hearts and minds of God's children—good and evil. Each soul must choose which of these forces it will adhere to, using its free will to do so. Those following the path of evil are called "The Followers of the Lie." Despite this battle, there is an underlying optimism in Zoroastrianism because it is understood that God and Good are destined from the start to win the battle.

The Gathas teaches that Wise God (*Ahura Mazda*) is the father of seven "Good Spirits" (*Amesha Spentas*), which help guide those who seek to align with Good; they are these: 1. The Holy Spirit; 2. Truthful Justice; 3. Righteous Thinking; 4. Devotion; 5. The "Desirable Dominion," which is a content state of peace and harmony; 6. Wholeness, and 7. Immortality. The first Good Spirit, "Holy Spirit," is an exact, literal translation of the Persian term *Spenta Mainyu*, which indicates that Jesus' later teachings about the importance of the Holy Spirit may have been known to his soul as far back as the sixth century BCE and relearned during his sojourn in Persia. Zoroastrianism also includes teachings that there will be a judgment of the soul at death and a resurrection of souls at the end times, when the "Desirable Dominion" is established forever.

After Persia, the Cayce readings say young Jesus went to India and was there for three years, studying under a teacher named *Arcahia*. He attended many schools in India, including the large ones in Jagannath and Benares.

In India he would have been trained and tested according to ancient Hinduism, which would be found in the sacred texts of the Vedas, Upanishads, and the Bhagavad-Gita ("The Lord's Song," ca. 200 BCE). He would have learned about Brahman and Atman. Brahman is an uncreated, eternal, infinite, transcendent, and all-embracing essence, which includes both being and non-being. It is the only true reality. Atman is the Self, the Logos, and the central consciousness of Beingness. In Western terms, it is the great "I AM" and is reflected in all the little "I ams." Atman gives self-consciousness to all beings. Atman is personal. Yet Atman exists within Brahman. Brahman is impersonal. Brahman is the One, the Whole, within which and through which everything exists. Brahman is also expressed in a Trinity: Brahma (the Creator, a personification of Brahman), Vishnu (the Preserver), and Shiva (the Destroyer). Jesus' teachings about the Trinity have some degree of harmony with ancient Hindu concepts.

Like Zoroastrianism, ancient Hinduism teaches that there is a battle raging between the good gods (*devas*) and the demoniac antigods (*asuras*). The cosmos (*sat*) is naturally governed by order and truth but is always in danger of being damaged or even destroyed by the powers of chaos (*asat*). During his time in India young Jesus would have also learned about reincarnation and karma.

The Cayce readings indicate that Jesus did as much teaching as learning and that much of what he experienced was in the form of testings rather than initiations, with the exception of his time in Egypt, where initiation was the primary experience. The "testings" were mostly conversations with the teachers and priests of these lands, just as he had experienced in the Temple in Jerusalem prior to departing. In *The Aquarian Gospel of Jesus Christ* by Levi, a writer who also received his information from the Akashic records, or what he called "God's Book of Remembrance," we find some detail on one incident which occurred during Jesus' time in India that may be an example of these testings. It is in chapter 29 of *The Aquarian Gospel* and goes like this:

Among Benares' temple priests was one, a guest, Ajainan, from Lahore. By merchant men Ajainin heard about the Jewish boy, about his words of wisdom, and he girt himself and journeyed from Lahore that he might see the boy, and hear him speak. The Brahmic priests did not accept the truth that Jesus brought, and they were angered much by what he said at the Udraka feast. But they had never seen the boy, and they desired much to hear him speak, and they invited him to be a temple guest. But Jesus said to them, "The light is most abundant, and it shines for all; if you would see the light come to the light. If you would hear the message that the Holy One has given me to give to men, come unto me." Now, when the priests were told what Jesus said they were enraged. Ajainin did not share their wrath, and he sent forth another messenger with costly gifts to Jesus at the farmer's home; he sent this message with the gifts: "I pray you master, listen to my words; The Brahmic law forbids that any priest shall go into the home of any one of low estate; but you can come to us; And I am sure these priests will gladly hear you speak. I pray that you will come and dine with us this day." And Jesus said, "The Holy One regards all men alike; the dwelling of my host is good enough for any council of the sons of men. If pride of cast keeps you away, you are not worthy of the light. My Father-God does not regard the laws of man. Your presents I return; you cannot buy the knowledge of the Lord with gold, or precious gifts." These words of Jesus angered more and more of the priests, and they began to plot and plan how they might drive him from the land. Ajainin did not join with them in plot and plan; he left the temple in the night and sought the home where Jesus dwelt. And Jesus said, "There is no night where shines the sun; I have no secret messages to give; in light all secrets are revealed." Ajainin said, "I came from faraway Lahore, that I might learn about this ancient wisdom, and this kingdom of the Holy One of which you speak. Where is the kingdom? where the king? Who are the subjects? what its laws?" And Jesus said, "This kingdom is not far away, but man with mortal eyes can see it not; it is within the heart. You need not seek the king in earth, or sea, or sky; he is not there, and yet is everywhere. He is the Christ of God; is universal love. The gate of this dominion is not high, and he who enters it must fall down on his knees. It is not wide, and none can carry carnal bundles through. The lower self must be transmuted into spirit-self; the body must be washed in living streams of purity." Ajainin asked, "Can I become a subject of this king?" And Jesus said, "You are yourself a king, and you may enter through the gate and be a subject of the King of kings. But you must lay aside your priestly robes; must cease to serve the Holy One for gold; must give your life, and all you have, in willing service to the sons of men." And Jesus said no more; Ajainin went his way; and while he could not comprehend the truth that Jesus spoke, he saw what he had never seen before. The realm of faith he never had explored; but in his heart the seeds of faith and universal brotherhood had found good soil. And as he journeyed to his home he seemed to sleep, to pass through darkest night, and when he woke the Sun of Righteousness had arisen; he had found the king. Now, in Benares Jesus tarried many days and taught.

From this account we can see that young Jesus was already experiencing the challenges of authorities, traditions, and prejudices, which he would also find in Judea during his coming ministry.

Since Cayce identifies one of the Wise Men as coming from "Tao Land," young Jesus would have learned about Taoism. Along with Confucianism, Taoism was one of the chief religions of ancient China. Taoism conveys a positive, active attitude toward the occult and metaphysical, in contrast to the agnostic, pragmatic Confucian traditions of social duty and austerity. The sacred texts of Taoism are *Tao-te Ching* (written by Lao-tzu), the *Chuang-tzu*, and the *Lieh-tzu*. Tao means "Way," referring to the way to fulfillment and immortality. According to Lao-tzu there is a Tao that is named and can be studied and practiced, but then there is a Tao that is unnamed and can be experienced only through an ecstasy that transcends normal reality. Taoism teaches that all multiplicity is returning, at least in consciousness, if not ultimately in reality, to a former oneness that it enjoyed before the creation. This can be mystically achieved in a moment of deep stillness, when all beingness returns to nonbeing, all action to nonaction. In Taoism there are again two forces in the world: those that disperse and those that unite; one of these sees only the manyness, the other sees the oneness. Yin and Yang would have been shown as two interwoven principles that manifest themselves in the separated external world but unite in the internal place of stillness.

Certainly in India and under the influence of those from Tao Land, young Jesus would have learned to meditate, transcending normal consciousness to experience the peace, oneness, and ecstasy of reunion with the Source of Life.

In chapter 36 of *The Aquarian Gospel* we have this depiction of young Jesus' time in Tao Land:

In Lassa of Tibet there was a master's temple, rich in manuscripts of ancient lore. The Indian sage had read these manuscripts, and he revealed to Jesus many of the secret lessons they contained; but Jesus wished to read them for himself. Now, Meng-ste, greatest sage of all the farther East, was in this temple of Tibet. The path across Emodus heights was difficult; but Jesus started on his way, and Vidyapati sent with him a trusted guide. And Vidyapati sent a message to Meng-ste, in which he told about the Hebrew sage, and spoke for him a welcome by the temple priests. Now, after many days, and perils great, the guide and Jesus reached the Lassa temple in Tibet. And Meng-ste opened wide the temple doors, and all the priests and masters gave a welcome to the Hebrew sage. And Jesus had access to all the sacred manuscripts, and, with the help of Meng-ste, read them all. And Meng-ste often talked with Jesus of the coming age, and of the sacred service best adapted to the people of the age. In Lassa Jesus did not teach. When he finished all his studies in the temple schools, he journeyed toward the West. In many villages he tarried for a time and taught. At last he reached the pass, and in the Ladak city, Leh, he was received with favor by the monks, the merchants, and the men of low estate. And in the monastery he abode, and taught; and then he sought the common people in the marts of trade; and there he taught. Not far away a woman lived, whose infant son was sick nigh unto death. The doctors had declared, "There is no hope; the child must die." The woman heard that Jesus was a teacher sent from God, and she believed that he had power to heal her son. And so she clasped the dying infant in her arms and ran with haste and asked to see the man of God. When Jesus saw her faith, he lifted up his eyes to heaven and said, "My Father-God, let power divine overshadow me, and let the Holy Breath fill full this child that it may live." And in the presence of the multitude he laid his hand upon the child and said, "Good woman you are blest; your faith has saved your son." And then the child was well. The people were astonished and they said, "This surely is the Holy One made flesh, for man alone cannot rebuke a fever thus and save a child from death." Then many of the people brought their sick, and Jesus spoke the Word, and they were healed. Among the Ladaks Jesus tarried many days; he taught them how to heal; how sins are blotted out, and how to make on earth a heaven of joy.

After Persia, India, and the Tao Land, young Jesus, according to Cayce, spent the rest of his time in Egypt, being trained and tested in Heliopolis (modern-day East Cairo) but taking his most significant initiation in Giza, inside the Great Pyramid. The readings say that John the Baptist was also there but in a different class. Cayce says that the "unifying of the teachings of many lands was brought together in Egypt; for that was the center from which there was to be the radial activity of influence in the Earth . . . until the new cycle begins" (2067-7). This "new cycle" is beginning now, in our time, and will lead to the much anticipated New Age, according to the Cayce readings.

In Egypt Jesus would have again found the theme of the Trinity: Ra, the Creator; Osiris, the Preserver and Judge; and Horus, the Savior. He would have again learned of the struggle between Good and Evil. He would have learned about the feminine and masculine forces that appear separate but actually compose a united whole in the higher state of consciousness. He would have learned about powerful feminine goddesses that helped save humanity from evil: Isis, Nephthys, Maat, Hathor, and others.

Cayce says that young Jesus reached the training level of priest in Egypt, and in the readings implies that he broke the King's Chamber sarcophagus during an initiation, as he overcame the power of death. This was apparently a foreshadowing of his victory later at the resurrection: "For, read ye, 'He was also crucified in Egypt'" (315-4). This would seem to be a comment on his initiation in Egypt as being like a crucifixion, a dying to self in order to resurrect as a result of making oneself in harmony and oneness with God, the source of all life. Another reading states: "There should be the reminding that, though He bowed under the burden of the Cross, though His blood was shed, though He entered into the tomb—through that power, that ability, that love as manifested in Himself among His fellow men He broke the bonds of death, proclaiming in that act that *there is no death* when the individual, the soul, has and does put its trust in Him." (5749-13)

In chapter 47 of *The Aquarian Gospel*, we have this account of Jesus' return to Egypt:

"Jesus came to Egypt land and all was well. He tarried not upon the coast; he went at once to Zoan, home of Elihu and Salome, who five and twenty years before had taught his mother in their sacred school.

And there was joy when [he] met these three. When last the son of Mary saw these sacred groves he was a babe; And now a man grown strong by buffeting of every kind; a teacher who had stirred the multitudes in many lands. And Jesus told the aged teachers all about his life; about his journeying in foreign lands; about the meetings with the masters and about his kind receptions by the multitudes. Elihu and Salome heard his story with delight; they lifted up their eyes to heaven and said, 'Our Father-God, let now thy servants go in peace, for we have seen the glory of the Lord; And we have talked with him, the messenger of love, and of the covenant of peace on earth, good will to men. Through him shall all the nations of the earth be blest; through him, Emmanuel' (meaning, God is among men). And Jesus stayed in Zoan many days; and then went forth unto the city of the sun, that men call Heliopolis, and sought admission to the temple of the sacred brotherhood. The council of the brotherhood convened, and Jesus stood before the hierophant; he answered all the questions that were asked with clearness and with power. The hierophant exclaimed, 'Rabboni of the rabbinate, why come you here? Your wisdom is the wisdom of the gods; why seek for wisdom in the halls of men?' And Jesus said, 'In every way of earth-life I would walk; in every hall of learning I would sit; the heights that any man has gained, these I would gain; What any man has suffered I would meet, that I may know the griefs, the disappointments and the sore temptations of my brother man; that I may know just how to succor those in need. I pray you, brothers, let me go into your dismal crypts; and I would pass the hardest of your tests.' The master said, 'Take then the vow of secret brotherhood.' And Jesus took the vow of secret brotherhood. Again the master spoke; he said, 'The greatest heights are gained by those who reach the greatest depths; and you shall reach the greatest depths.'"

The Aquarian Gospel records seven trials or tests that Jesus went through in his initiation into the Egyptian mystery school. They were these: 1. Test of Sincerity, in which victory over deceit was achieved; 2. Test of Justice; in which victory over "the phantoms of prejudice and treachery" were achieved; 3. Test of Faith, in which victory over the seduction of earthly wealth, honor, and fame were achieved; 4. Test of Philanthropy or Charity, in which victory over self-gratification was achieved; 5. Test of Heroism, in which victory over fear was achieved; 6. Test of Divine Love, in which victory over getting lost in carnal love was achieved; and 7. Test of Life in the Chamber of Death, in which Death no longer meant the end of one's true self, and consciousness of that true self lives beyond the physical body. Cayce's readings describe this last test as being an actual death of the body in the sarcophagus for a significant duration, becoming conscious in the worlds beyond this one, and then a return to resurrect the body and recall the whole process consciously, whereas Levi's account is much more a mental wrestling with human perspectives on death.

There are some non–Akashic sources for tales of young Jesus' journeys. And though they are questioned by some, they are worth presenting here. The first is Nicolas Notovitch who traveled throughout India, Tibet, and Afghanistan in the 1880s and wrote that while he was recovering from an injury at the Buddhist monastery Himis, in Ledak (then in the western region of Tibet but today is in the northernmost part of India), he was shown a copy of a manuscript titled *The Life of Saint Issa*. Issa, Notovitch came to understand, was a Buddhist equivalent of the name Jesus. He was told that the manuscript was about a "saint" from the West who had been revered by Hindus and Buddhists. He managed to have the manuscript read to him aloud, in translation, of course. To his amazement, it contained the whole story of Jesus' life, from twelve years of age until thirty. Notovitch said that the monks told him that the original of this copy was located in the monastery on Mount Marbour, near Lhasa, with other copies at several of the country's other major monasteries. After the publication of his book in 1894, *The Unknown Life of Jesus Christ*, Notovitch came under much criticism. Orientalist Max Müller, editor of Sacred Books of the East series, argued that such an honored work as Notovitch described would surely have been included in the canon of Tibetan books, the *Kanjur* and the *Tanjur*. But it wasn't.

Notovitch's manuscript (reprinted in my book *A Broader View of Jesus Christ*, available at Amazon.com) contains an amazing story of the journeys of young Jesus to many of India's classic centers of spiritual thought and practice. Janet Bock and her husband, Richard, traveled to India to retrace the young Jesus' journey as Notovitch had revealed it. Bock's book on their journeys came out in 1980, titled *The Jesus Mystery of the Lost Years and Unknown Travels*.

Thirty-five years after Notovitch, Swami Abhedananda went to Himis in 1922 and saw the manuscript and wrote about it in his Bengali book of travels, *Kashmiri O Tibbetti*, meaning "Journey to Kashmir and Tibet." Swami Abhedananda later wrote another book titled *Was Christ a Yogi?* In this book the Swami wrote that Christ was more than a yogi and believed that his God was also the God of Hinduism, Jainism, and Buddhism.

Nicholas Roerich, a mystic painter, visited Central Asia in search of the lost city of Shambhala and other mysteries. He, too, visited Himis. In 1925, he recorded what he claimed were extracts of popular tales about Saint Issa as well as related material from a 1500-year-old Tibetan manuscript. Some question his findings, based on the age of this manuscript being nearly four hundred years after the events it supposedly records. Of course, a Bible today is a manuscript recording events that occurred two thousand years ago yet is no less valued as representative of the original story.

In 1939 Dr. Elisabeth Caspari, a member of the Mazdaznan sect, associated with Zoroastrianism, journeyed into Tibet with some female friends and attended a festival at the Himis monastery. One day during their stay, she reports that the librarian and two other monks showed the ladies three Buddhist books made of sheets of parchment, sandwiched between two pieces of wood, and wrapped in brocades. The librarian told the women that these books say your Jesus was here.

Unfortunately, no one brought forth anything that resembles a genuine Tibetan manuscript containing the story of Saint Issa. Since 1947 Tibet and its monasteries have been under the control of Communist China. Therefore, the legend and the Tibetan manuscripts remain a fascinating, unsubstantiated story.

Chapter 6

Edgar Cayce's Discourses on the Essenes

The Edgar Cayce discourses were called "readings" because Cayce was mentally "reading" what has been termed the Book of Life, the Book of Remembrance, and the Akashic record. He would lie down with his hands over his third eye (forehead) until he saw a *light*, then he would move his hands over his solar plexus and begin to go into a deep trance. In order to proceed with a reading, he needed a *directive suggestion*, which was usually given by the "conductor" of the reading, typically his wife Gertrude Evans Cayce or his eldest son Hugh Lynn Cayce. She would watch for his breathing to get deeper and for rapid eye movement (REM); then she would give him the directive suggestion. It usually began with something like this: "You will have before you the records of..." and then once the reading was done he had to have another directive suggestion to wake up. So deep were these trances that on one sad occasion a doctor attempting to study the Cayce phenomenon torn his little finger's nail off and noted that Cayce did even flinch—that is, until he woke up! During most reading sessions Cayce was so tuned into what was needed to get the reading recorded properly that he could actually pause to give his stenographer the correct spelling of a word or name. On occasions when they used a recording device that could only hold fifteen minutes of voice recordings, he actually stopped in mid–sentence while the full recording disk was replaced and immediately began again exactly where he left off when the new disk was ready.

Cayce's readings can be difficult to read because when in these trances he spoke in a King–James–Bible English, with *thee, thy, thou, thine, knowest, endureth, leaveneth,* and the like. Additionally, he used unusual syntax and sentence structure, and often had multiple subjects in one paragraph, making it difficult to be sure which he was speaking about. But if one reads *slowly* and *reflectively,* one can grasp the message and meaning. Where you find words in *italicized* letters, it is when the volume of his voice increased, as he was emphasizing the words. His stenographer Gladys told me that she would simply all–cap the word—today we would italicize the word. Where you see "(Life Reading Suggestion)" it means that in the trance–state Cayce received a standard suggestion to give a reading, but the whole suggestion was not recorded. There were two distinct types of readings: a Health Reading, sought for improving the condition of one's body, and a Life Reading, sought for gaining insight into one's soul journey. The Health Readings were amazing because it was as if Cayce's deeper mind was a modern medical laboratory that could determine the condition of the body in every detail, even the history of the body, noting injuries that may have happened years earlier and their effects on the body during the reading! In a Life Reading Cayce would begin by giving the soul's celestial activities, their so–called "planetary sojourns" between earth incarnations. Then he would follow these with their past lives in the "earth plane." In most all cases, Cayce gave only a few of the incarnations that the soul had, those most closely influencing the soul's present incarnation.

Where you see "GC," that is Edgar's wife Gertrude, and "HLC" is his son Hugh Lynn acting as the conductor of the reading and giving the opening and closing suggestions, as well as asking the questions during the reading. Of course "EC" is Edgar Cayce.

Once the suggestion for a Life Reading was given, Cayce followed to the Hall of Records the light he had initially seen when his hands were on his forehead and received the Book of Life of the individual seeking the reading. The keeper of the records would show him what could and could not be read. If it was a Health Reading, it was given if the person's entire organism was accessible to Cayce's mind. He would often give the condition of the nervous systems, the circulatory and the elimination systems, the chemistry of the body, and so on. If asked about something specific in the body, it was as if he could see inside and perceive the entire complexity of the body's functioning. Here's an example:

(Q) Mr. Cayce, the body wants to know whether you find gall stones?
(A) We do not find gall stones. There are improper secretions at times in the system from the functioning of the liver. With these properties we have given we are to relieve this condition through the excretory system, both in the liver and the kidneys where we find the same sedimentary forces that are, at times, left in the system. In the kidneys we find more expression at times through the bladder, that is, the urinary canal, you see. With the mind correctly governed and with the properties to give the correct incentive to the functioning of the digestive tract or with the proper balance created through the alimentary canal, we will find the body sufficiently balanced to throw off all of this refuse matter from the system. Do that.   1010-1

All the personal names of the people getting these readings have been replaced with numbers for reasons of privacy. However, there is a little profile of the person at the top of each reading. An example is: "F 62 (Widow, Protestant)" for Mrs. 1391. The dash number following her name–replacement number indicates which of her readings it is, "–1" being her first reading and "–12" indicating her twelfth reading.

The following Cayce readings focus on souls who were once members of the Essenes and had reincarnated during Cayce lifetime and who got one or more of his famous readings. I've presented the entire reading so that you might get the full perspective of a soul's journey—in hopes that this helps each of us gain a sense of our own soul's journey.

The first reading is specific to the Essenes, but the subsequent discourses are past–life readings for individual souls who were once incarnate members of the Essenes or worked closely with them.

I have left the actual transcription in its original format (with the exception of italicizing and lower casing the words written in all caps) to give you an exact depiction of the filed discourses in the vaults at

Edgar Cayce's center in Virginia Beach, Virginia, known as the Association for Research and Enlightenment, or A.R.E. The entire collection of Cayce readings is available online to members of the Association at EdgarCayce.org and for sale to anyone on a CD–ROM at AREcatalog.com.

To help us I make some "My note" comments as we go through the readings.

TEXT OF READING 254-109

This psychic reading given by Edgar Cayce at the office of the Association, Arctic Crescent, Virginia Beach, Virginia, this 20th day of May, 1941, in accordance with request made by the Manager of the Association, Mr. Hugh Lynn Cayce.

PRESENT

Edgar Cayce; Hugh Lynn Cayce, Conductor; Gladys Davis, Steno.

READING

Time of Reading 11:20 to 11:45 A. M. Eastern Standard Time. . . . , Va.

HLC: You will have before you the work of the Association in preparing and presenting a pamphlet on information given through this channel, in life readings and general readings, pertaining to the Essenes' preparation for the coming of Jesus. The writing of this pamphlet is in the hands of Enid S. Smith of 503 West 121st Street, New York, City. You will answer the questions, as I ask them:

EC: Yes, we have the work, the policies and the purposes of the Association for Research and Enlightenment, Incorporated, together with information which has been supplied through this channel, Edgar Cayce; also the work as done on same by Enid S. Smith.

As we find, in the main this has been very well done. There may be made one suggestion as to attempting to make that presented through these sources conform to that which is already a part of the public record.

Draw a parallel, rather than attempting to so word or phrase such paragraphs as to conform. One would be rather the introduction to the other.

Ready for questions.

(Q) Comment fully on just what the purpose, objectives, and general tone of this pamphlet should be.

(A) This should be the tone:

It is generally conceded by those who are students—in the Christian faith as well as in many other phases of spiritual evolution—that there is the expectancy of a new order, or a fulfilling of or a return to those activities that may bring about the time for that redemption of the world; in a return or in an acknowledgement of that as the basis of the individual instruction or direction.

Then, this pamphlet or paper should give to others an insight as to what and how there was the physical, mental, and spiritual attitude of that group; as to how those individuals so well acted their part, and yet not becoming known in that presented.

So, this may enable individuals and groups to so prepare themselves as to be channels through which the more perfect way may be seen.

(Q) What is the correct meaning of the term "Essene"?

(A) Expectancy.

(Q) Was the main purpose of the Essenes to raise up people who would be fit channels for the birth of the Messiah who later would be sent out into the world to represent their Brotherhood?

(A) The individual preparation was the first purpose. The being sent out into the world was secondary. Only a very few held to the idea of the realization in organization, other than that which would come with the Messiah's pronouncements. [**My note:** Here he is stating that very few of the Essenes had thought much beyond the challenge of preparing the way for the Messiah to enter this world. There was little to no thought of organizing an outreach network to bring the Messiah's message to the world.]

(Q) Were the Essenes called at various times and places Nazarites, School of the Prophets, Hasidees, Therapeutae, Nazarenes, and were they a branch of the Great White Brotherhood, starting in Egypt and taking as members Gentiles and Jews alike?

(A) In general, yes. Specifically, not altogether. They were known at times as some of these; or the Nazarites were a branch or a *thought* of same, see? [**My note:** There will be clarity on this in the chapter on young Jesus' Essene teacher.] Just as in the present one would say that any denomination by name is a branch of the Christian-Protestant faith, see? So were those of the various groups, though their purpose was of the first foundations of the prophets as established, or as understood from the school of prophets, by Elijah; and propagated and studied through the things begun by Samuel.

The movement was *not* an Egyptian one, though *adopted* by those in another period—or an earlier period—and made a part of the whole movement.

They took Jews and Gentiles alike as members—yes.

[**My note:** As I wrote earlier, in the Bible there are over twenty mentions of the School of the Prophets and groups of prophets working as a community. Clearly there had been developed and maintained a large community of prophets and prophetesses for hundreds of years in Israel. The term *prophet* is difficult to define but since the noun "prophet" comes from the Hebrew verb *naba*, meaning "to bubble up" or "boil forth," we may use this definition: A prophet is one who enters heightened states of awareness and pours forth words from divine inspiration.]

Now back to the reading:

(Q) Please describe the associate membership of the women in the Essene brotherhood, telling what privileges and restrictions they had, how they joined the Order, and what their life and work was.

(A) This was the beginning of the period where women were considered as equals with the men in their activities, in their abilities to formulate, to live, to be, channels. They joined by dedication—usually by their parents. It was a freewill thing all the way through, but they were restricted only in the matter of certain foods and certain associations in various periods—which referred to the sex, as well as to the food or drink.

(Q) How did Mary and Joseph first come in contact with the Essenes and what was their preparation for the coming of Jesus?

(A) As indicated, by being dedicated by their parents.

(Q) Please describe the process of selection and training of those set aside as holy women such as Mary, Editha [587], and others as a possible mother for the Christ. How were they chosen, were they mated, and what was their life and work while they waited in the Temple? [**My note:** Cayce had already given readings about how the Essenes had carefully read Genesis and how the redemption of the Fall in the Garden would begin with a woman conceiving the redeemer, and the redeemer would subdue the serpent energy that had gotten them in trouble. Therefore, the Essenes were gathering select girls in their temple at Mount Carmel and putting them through training and tests to determine which of them might actually conceive the promised messiah. Cayce further explained that Anna, Mary's mother, had come to the temple pregnant yet had not yet had sex with a man. They took Anna in, and when she gave birth to a girl, there was a discussion that ended in a decision to keep the girl since she might be, as some thought the messiah would be, the immaculately conceived feminine messiah who would eventually conceive through the Holy Spirit the masculine messiah.]

(A) They were first dedicated and then there was the choice of the individual through the growths, as to whether they would be merely channels for general services. For, these were chosen for special services at various times; as were the twelve [finalists] chosen at the time, which may be used as an illustration. Remember, these came down from the periods when the school had begun, you see.

When there were the activities in which there were to be the cleansings through which bodies were to become channels for the new race, or the new preparation, these then were restricted—of course—as to certain associations, developments in associations, activities and the like. We are speaking here of the twelve women, you see—and all of the women from the very beginning who were dedicated as channels for the new race, see?

Hence the group we refer to here as the Essenes, which was the outgrowth of the periods of preparations from the teachings by Melchizedek, as propagated by Elijah and Elisha and Samuel. These were set aside for preserving themselves in direct line of choice for the offering of themselves as channels through which there might come the new or the divine origin, see?

Their life and work during such periods of preparation were given to alms, good deeds, missionary activities—as would be termed today.

(Q) Please tell of the contacts of Thesea [2067], Herod's third wife, with the Essenes, her meeting with one of the Essene Wise Men, and what were the names of the two wives preceding her?

(A) There was the knowledge of same through the giving of information by one of those in the household who had been so set aside for active service. Through the manner and conduct of life of that individual, and the associations and activities, the entity gained knowledge of that group's activities. [**My note:** Herod's third wife, Thesea, had a handmaid who was secretly an Essene, and she helped Thesea meet secretly with Essene teachers, as Thesea was moved to learn spiritual truths.]

(Q) Please describe the Essene wedding, in temple, of Mary and Joseph, giving the form of ceremony and customs at that time.

(A) This followed very closely the form outlined in Ruth. It was not in any way a supplanting but a cherishing of the sincerity of purpose in the activities of individuals.

[**My note:** I shared a little of this in the first chapter of this book, but since we are going over the entire reading, and seeking greater detail, I'll go over this again here. Cayce's comment about the biblical book of Ruth being an outline of the wedding ceremony and customs is a bit difficult to explain. The young widow Ruth is indeed the ancestor of Mary's Joseph, for Ruth is the great-grandmother of David, and Joseph was of the House of David's lineage. But there is no wedding ceremony described in the book of Ruth. We learn that the young widow Ruth lies at the feet of sleeping Boaz, a good man whom, pushed by Naomi, Ruth seeks to be her next husband. She eventually marries and has the boy child who in turn leads to the birth of David and finally to Joseph. But here's a possible connection, and Cayce is going to mention this in the next paragraph: It was the tradition of the followers of Moses that the nearest of kin (not by blood but by family connections, yet a *relative*) take in care and marriage young women of their tribe (Leviticus 25:25-55). Boaz indicated his desire to marry Ruth, calling her a "woman of noble character." But there was a relative with a stronger claim to Ruth's hand (per the Mosaic requirements in Deuteronomy 25:7-9), so Boaz had to resolve that first before he could legally marry Ruth. Cayce indicates in this paragraph of his reading that *Mary's* nearest of kin was an old man, Joseph the carpenter, not a normally acceptable mate for a new marriage to a very young girl.] Back to the reading:

When there was to be the association, or the wedding of Joseph and Mary—Mary having been chosen as the channel by the activities indicated upon the stair, by the hovering of the angel, the enunciation to Anna and to Judy [1472—Judy is explained in detail in a later chapter] and to the rest of those in charge of the preparations at that time—then there was to be sought out the nearer of kin, though *not* kin in the blood relationships. Thus the lot fell upon Joseph, though he was a much older man compared to the age ordinarily attributed to Mary in the period. Thus there followed the regular ritual in the temple. For, remember, the Jews were not refrained [by the Romans] from following their rituals. Those of the other groups, as the Egyptians or the Parthians, were not refrained from following the customs to which they had been trained; which were not carried on in the Jewish temple but rather in the general meeting place of the Essenes as a body-organization.

(Q) What parts of the historical material prepared by Enid Smith should be emphasized in the pamphlet on Essenism, and how best can this material be handled in connection with the Essene material from the life readings?

(A) As indicated. By paralleling.

(Q) Are there any other suggestions at this time regarding this pamphlet?

(A) Make the ceremonies a very beautiful thing—as may be drawn from how there is the meeting of individuals, and thus the announcing of the privileges of both parents concerning the wedding of those in the Essene group, whether Jew or those of other faiths or other understandings. Make of this a beautiful thing, not as of being "sold."

We are through for the present.

Copy to Hugh Lynn Cayce for Dr. Enid Smith [Ph.D.], Ass'n File

This next Cayce discourse is a "Life Reading" for a woman with a past life as an Essene. She is an especially spiritual soul, and Cayce points out how her approach to life has helped her to be healthy and enlightened, but now she has to be careful not to judge too harshly others who have not done so well with their free will and soul growth.

TEXT OF READING 1391-1
F 62 (Widow, Protestant)

This Psychic Reading given by Edgar Cayce at his home on Arctic Crescent, Virginia Beach, Va., this 22nd day of June, 1937, in accordance with request made by the self—Mrs. [1391], new Active Member of the Ass'n for Research & Enlightenment, Inc., recommended by Mr. [1196].

PRESENT

Edgar Cayce; Gertrude Cayce, Conductor; Gladys Davis, Steno. Mrs. [1391].

READING

Born April 12, 1875, in Greenville, Alabama.

Time of Reading 10:50 to 11:45 A. M. Eastern Standard Time . . . , Alabama.

(Life Reading Suggestion)

EC: Yes.

We have the records here of that entity known as or called [1391].

In giving the interpretations of the records here, we find the astrological aspects very little—from the ordinary standpoint—in keeping with that which has been manifested or developed through the entity's experiences or sojourns; or they have been altered by the activities and manifestations of the entity in the material plane.

From the astrological sojourns we find the mental or innate urges, while from the material or earthly sojourns we find the emotions of the entity.

As we find in drawing the comparisons of those influences:

The entity is one very highly developed in the mental and spiritual aspects of materiality, as well as in the seeking.

Would that all would gain much as the entity has (and apparently as a natural consequence for the entity's material consciousness) that it is the continuous and continued *"try"* that is counted—as in the soul development—for spiritual righteousness.

Only those who become distorted, disturbed, and attempt to express or manifest their own ego, become the more confused—in not having their own way.

As to the experience of the entity from the astrological and from the earthly sojourn, the entity's entrance into the material plane as for the physical birth was in the evening, while the spiritual birth was close to what is called the witching hour. [**My note:** midnight.]

Hence the entity has at times been considered by some a little stubborn, hard-headed, determined; yet these have become in the application of the *"try"* for spiritual understanding, spiritual concept, rather stepping-stones than stumbling-blocks—as so oft experienced by many.

In the activities then, we find that while in the early experiences in the earth the entity was one tending towards being physically weak, having periods when there were those besetting influences of dis-ease, disturbances of varied natures, the taking hold—the determination to be of a purposefulness, of a worth while and a practical application of the spiritual laws in the mental and material plane—has made for rather a resistance, a strong body, mentally, physically.

Hence there only needs to be the holding to those tenets as for nature and God to care for the physical needs to have the opportunities for ministering, as has been given in the promise which the entity has held to, "Honor thy father and thy mother, that thy days may be long in the land which the Lord thy God giveth thee."

These have been practical experiences in the activities of the entity, and are thus enjoined as a part of the entity's experience.

Judge then not too harshly those who have not gained an insight into the fact that "The laws of the Lord are perfect, converting the soul" if they will be applied in the *"try"* in the experience of the material life.

In the astrological aspects we find Venus, Jupiter, Mercury, Mars, Saturn as the ruling forces; or the experiences of sojourn in the entity's activity; and, as has been indicated, these do not run true to form for the position, but rather in the terms and the inclinations that have been indicated by the various sojourns of the entity in the activity of that accredited to each of the planetary environs given.

[**My note:** Cayce's readings teach that souls are active between physical incarnations in realms associated with the planets in the solar system. Not in the three-dimensional reality but in fourth and fifth dimensional states of existence associated with the physical planets. It is as though the solar system is a soul *university* and each of the planets is a *college* within that university, and ancient astrology's description of each planet's influence is that college's main lesson. Thus, Mercury would be the mental lessons and development, Venus would be love, friendships, creativity, and beauty, and the planets would continue according to classical astrological descriptions. You will also notice that Cayce sees how planetary movements during one's incarnation bring these influences around again, often referred to as "transiting influences."]

Hence in Venus while adverse in some experiences, the friendships, the little kindnesses shown by the entity have sealed, have made the brighter spots, the brighter periods in the experience of the entity.

And as indicated by the Jupiterian influence as it comes in the latter portion especially of this coming year and the present year, there will be more changes, more associations of the entity with large groups, and greater will be the activities of the entity in influencing the larger groups; while in the greater portion of the entity's experience thus far the activities in the mental and spiritual have been rather to the individual than the group or the masses.

In Mercury we find that seeking for high mental aspirations, high mental abilities. Hence the entity becomes more and more intuitive in its experience, in its associations, in its studies of activities, experiences or associations with others.

Hence the first impressions—if the entity closes the consciousness (that is, the consciousness of the physical nature)—are the more lasting. For as indicated through those benevolent influences of the Venus experiences and Venus sojourns, in love divine, in love as in friendships—if one would find love, one must show self lovely; if one would have friends, one must show self friendly. For that you sow, that you reap. For into the soil of human experience go the activities of every individual in its dealings, its associations, and its reactions to the mental, the material, and the spiritual aspect of every soul's experience.

For not only in self as the study of self is there the understanding and the comprehending of the experiences of others but also in the study of the spiritual self and the spiritual application in the material world there is the gaining for the individual of a greater consciousness and a greater understanding of Infinity in its relationships. [**My note:** From Cayce's perspective, gaining an awareness of the finite (our normal reality) as well as the infinite (the greater reality) was important to soul growth.]

For as each soul is in the image of the Maker, so do the activities find more and more that there must be seen, there must be reflected not only in self but seen in the mind and the heart and the soul of others that you would worship in your Creator.

As to the appearances in the earth, these we find rather of a varied nature; some queenly, some lowly, some a gaining, some a stumbling. These have been, then, sojourns *full* of experience for this, what may be termed an old soul in those activities in the various phases of human and mental experiences.

[**My note:** According to Cayce's readings, all souls were created at once, in a "Big Bang" like expression from out of the Infinite, Universal Consciousness of the Creative Forces, or God. However, souls who had been very active and involved in many experiences he nicknamed "old souls," while those that had not used their free will as much, especially when it came to earth incarnations, were "new souls," meaning to new to this activity.]

Before this we find the entity was in the land of the present nativity [Alabama], during those periods when there were the first of the settlings in the land from those called the French peoples who came to this land and were active as settlers.

The entity then was of the house of royalty, as would be termed, or of those in authority in relationships with royalty; and the pioneering days or periods in the land made for experiences and activities that brought an understanding of nature in the *raw* as might be termed in common parlance—and nature in the raw in its closeness to the divine.

For as has been oft indicated, there is such a thin veil existing between the ridiculous and the sublime, the spiritual and the divine, the material and the mental, that there is little wonder that man oft in his groping misinterprets, misconstrues, misunderstands those influences in the experiences of others.

And the entity in that experience (as has been and is so oft a part of man's development) regarded too much "What will people say?"

This lesson the entity earned and learned during that sojourn, as Florence Boetella; and in those experiences as indicated the entity gained through the application of self to meet the needs of the material and the mental and the spiritual life of individuals—as a teacher, as a minister.

Hence in the experience of the entity in the present many have oft come and will come to the entity for counsel, for advice; for those ways in which there may be help to the young, help to the developing, help to the expectant ones, help to those who are disturbed in body, in mind, and in the fields of separations of the not seen.

These (the fields of separations of the not seen) the entity has met, has conquered in part. Hold fast to that, then, which is good; and you will find that in those periods when there is the evening sum or sun of life in this experience, there will be the greater joy and the greater beauty and the greater expectancy—because of the more and more expectancy in the *great undertaking,* the *great unknown,* to so many.

Yet if we learn more and more that separations are only walking through the rooms as it were of God's house, we become—in these separations, in these experiences—aware of what is meant by that which has been and is the law, as from the beginning; "Know O ye peoples, the Lord thy God is *one!*"

And ye must be one—one with another, one with Him—if ye would be, as indeed ye are, corpuscles in the *life flow* of thy Redeemer!

Before that we find the entity was in that land of *the nativity,* when the Master walked in the earth, when there were those who gathered to listen, to interpret, to seek not only physical but mental and spiritual relief and understanding.

The entity then was among those of the holy women and those in close acquaintanceship with many who were the teachers or the apostles or the disciples, many of those women—as Mary, Martha, Elizabeth; all of these were as friends, yea companions of the entity during the experience.

For the entity then was in that capacity as one of the holy women who ministered in the temple service and in the preparation of those who dedicated their lives for individual activity during the sojourn.

The entity was then what would be termed in the present, in some organizations, as a Sister Superior, or an officer as it were in those of the Essenes and their preparations.

Hence we find the entity then giving, giving, ministering, encouraging, making for the greater activities; and making for those encouraging experiences oft in the lives of the Disciples; coming in contact with the Master oft in the ways between Bethany, Galilee, Jerusalem. For, as indicated, the entity kept the school on the way above Emmaus to the way that "goeth down towards Jericho" and towards the northernmost coast from Jerusalem.

The name then was Eloise, and the entity blessed many of those who came to seek to know the teachings, the ways, the mysteries, the understandings; for the entity had been trained in the schools of those that were of the prophets and prophetesses, and the entity was indeed a prophetess in those experiences—thus gained throughout.

Hence the stories of the experiences and activities of the Holy Women mean oft more to the entity, through the intuitive forces, through the impelling force of *good* in relationships to others.

[**My note:** Eloise would have known Edgar Cayce's soul in that Essene lifetime because Cayce incarnated during this time as Lucius of Cyrene of Grecian and Roman parentage—his mother was Jewish but his father was Greco-Roman. The readings indicate that Lucius' young wife studied with the holy women (Mary, the mother of Jesus, Judy, Elizabeth, and others that Eloise knew and companioned). Presumably his young wife taught her husband during their private moments together. Lucius was chosen to be among the initial seventy disciples, which was a great honor. And later, after Jesus' ascension to the Father, he grew to become the Bishop of the Jewish-Christian "church" of Laodicea in Asia Minor (modern-day Turkey). His full reading on this life is coming shortly.]

So we will find that in this experience the greater gain, the greater promise, the greater satisfaction, the greater hope comes to the entity in its ministering to others; not in the way of an overflow of sympathy, not in the way of laudation of any particular activity, but the encouragings here, the aiding there, in encouraging words, encouraging deeds, that they press on.

For all, as has been given, are as one before the throne of grace and mercy and peace and justice. For God is not the respecter of persons or of places or positions.

For to fulfill that purpose for which an entity, a being, has manifested in matter is the greater service that can possibly be rendered.

Is the oak the lord over the vine? Is the Jimson beset before the tomato? Are the grassy roots ashamed of their flower beside the rose?

All those forces in nature are fulfilling rather those purposes to which their Maker, their Creator, has called them into being.

Man—as the entity taught, as the entity gave—is in that position where he may gain the greater lesson from nature, and the creatures in the natural world; they each fulfilling their purpose, singing their song, filling the air with their perfume, that they—too—may honor and praise their Creator; though in their humble way in comparison to some, they each in their *own* humble way are fulfilling that for which they were called into being, reflecting—as each soul, as each man and each woman should do in their particular sphere—*their* concept of their Maker!

This is the purpose—as the entity taught; this is the purpose the entity may find in giving its comfort, in giving the cheery word, in giving the lessons to those in all walks of life.

Fulfill thy purpose in thy relationship to thy Maker, not to any individual, not to any group, not to any organization, not to any activity outside of self than to thy Creator!

For it is the reflection of Him.

Before that, then, we find the entity was in the "city in the hills and the plains" during those experiences when there were those turmoils from the early activities of those who rebelled against the Persian activities from which the leader Uhjltd [pronounced, yool-t] had ridden. [**My note:** Uhjltd was an incarnation of Edgar Cayce. (294-143)]

The entity was among those of a portion of the household of Uhjltd; hence a cousin to that leader. The entity espoused the cause of the leader and held fast through those periods of oppression, through those activities of Edssi, and the other leaders that brought the closer activity in the healing of the body. As the entity brought others for the physical healing, so the entity gained in those activities of the mental and spiritual understanding.

Hence we find the entity then in the name Iradia making for a healing, a counseling with those of many customs, those of many lands, those of many variations of thought brought into a unison—to the holding to that which is good; for good is from the all good, which is God.

Hence the same lessons and the activities the entity gained, the entity lost. For when those turmoils came from the beauties from Greece, with the temptations that arose, the entity became entangled with those of that particular undertaking. Yet in the latter portion of the experience the entity again turned to those tenets that made for the experiences and the activities in the developing of those periods for the peoples of many lands.

Before that we find the entity was in the Atlantean land when there were those journeyings from same into the Egyptian land, and into the various periods of interpretations. [**My note:** Here again this soul connects with Edgar Cayce's soul journeys, for he also had a past life as a priest in Egypt when the Atlanteans arrived. (294-147)]

The entity aided not only Ra but those of the land of Saneid, those from the land of Wu, those from the Pyrenees and those from the Carpathian land. All of these were a part of the activity of the entity, as the princess of those peoples as they came from the Atlantean land and gave the interpretation of the Law of One as reflected in the mechanical, the commercial, the spiritual, the theological activities of the experiences of individuals.

Then the entity was in the name Estehr-Esthar, and its experience was more active than many of the peoples; for the burdens of the many activities fell upon the entity in the interpretation of those various tenets and truths.

And it might be said that the entity was the more active in bringing about that period in the experience of the earth when there were the closer walks with the sons of God by the sons of men, through the peace wrought by the allaying of the fears of those in many varied lands.

As to the abilities of the entity in the present, then, and that to which it may attain, and how:

First, study to show thyself approved unto thy consciousness of the in-dwelling of God in Christ in thee; rightly divining (and dividing) the words of truth, putting proper evaluation upon the experiences in the activities of individuals and groups; keeping self unspotted from that which ye would question in another.

Minister to those in many places; gentleness, kindness, patience. For in patience ye become aware of thy relationship to Patience as shown by thy Savior, with a world that might have been eradicated by only a word—yet He wept, rather than found fault.

Do thou likewise. Weep with those that weep; rejoice with those that do rejoice; for in humbleness, in patience, ye may find thy true relationship to thy fellow man; and in thy ministry to thy brethren, to thy neighbors, yea to thy enemies, ye show forth thy concept, ye show forth the love ye have of thy Lord till He comes again!

Ready for questions.

(Q) Should I continue to live at present location, . . . , Ala.?

(A) For the present. As the various activities in thy studies and thy re-lationships develop, in thy ability to minister in thy relationships, the ways will be opened for changes.

(Q) Is there anything of value on my plantation in . . . , Ala., and will I be able to profit by it?

(A) This we find far afield from that which has been indicated. This should be approached rather from another angle.

(Q) Give me some advice to help to make more happiness in my home life.

(A) As that as has been given; study to show thyself approved, not find-ing fault, even as thy Master did not; making the proper evaluations in the experience of self and in others. These keep and make for harmonies—if reasoned together.

Let the ways of mercy and justice, as ye meted it to those in Galilee, to those in Bethsaida, to those in Bethany, as ye gave counsel to those in the days when turmoils were arising and those oppressions from the political forces made for dissensions, be thy counsel in the present.

And this has been given in ways that, studied, meditated upon, will open new vistas of possibilities to the self.

We are through for the present.

Copy to Self, Ass'n file

The following is another reading covering information needed for a pamphlet being prepared by some members of the A.R.E. for publication. It's mostly a Q & A session and contains some interesting and enlightening details about the time of the Essenes. Remember, we have already learned that Mrs. 2067 was the reincarnation of Herod's third wife, Thesea, who secretly met with the Essenes to learn the deeper truths, and it is *she* who is getting the following reading.

TEXT OF READING 2067-7
F 53 (Teacher, Quaker, Spiritualist)

This Psychic Reading given by Edgar Cayce at the office of the Association, Arctic Crescent, Virginia Beach, Va., this 25th day of June, 1941, in accordance with request made by the self—Dr. [2067], Associate Member of the Ass'n for Research & Enlightenment, Inc.

PRESENT

Edgar Cayce; Gertrude Cayce, Conductor; Gladys Davis, Steno. Dr. [2067], Helen Ellington, Esther Wynne, Florence Edmonds, Ruth LeNoir and Frances Y. Morrow.

READING

Time of Reading 3:30 to 4:10 P. M. Eastern Standard Time.

GC: You will have before you the material extracted from the Life Readings covering the period of Jesus' ministry, and being prepared by [2067] present in this room, for pamphlet presentation. You will answer the questions which have been prepared regarding this work.

EC: Yes, we have the desires and the hopes, with the information that has been gathered. Ready for questions.

(Q) Can you suggest an appropriate title for the Christ Ministry Pamphlet?

(A) This depends much upon the manner in which the information is compiled; as to its purpose, as to its completeness and as to that it may accomplish. It would be best to leave this with those who would publish same.

(Q) The excerpts from the Readings group themselves around the following topics: A. Preparation of Jesus, His early life and training; B. Events connected with the "holy women"; C. Events connected with the "holy family"; D. Events connected with John Baptist and family; E. Events connected with the home at Bethany; F. Verification and supplementary material to Gospel stories; G. Jesus' blessing of numerous children; H. Events connected with disciples, apostles, bishops of early churches; I. Rulers, governors, Roman officers connected with ministry of Jesus; J. Additional events, not in Gospels, of especial interest to history; [and] K. Philosophic teachings of great value to the Christian (new light). Would you include the major part of this material in one pamphlet, or how would you suggest it be arranged?

(A) *Again*—what is the purpose? What is to be gained from this, and that has not been accomplished in other data of similar nature? Is it for the propagation of propaganda for a group that is attempting to make a cult, or is it to supply the needed stimuli to all for service in the channels in which they find themselves drawn, for one or another cause? This depends, then, upon that phase of the approach—as to how or in what manner this would be prepared for distribution.

(Q) Please suggest to [2067] the purpose of the pamphlet and the especial timeliness of the pamphlet (Christ Ministry) assigned to her.

(A) Why would you suggest a purpose for preparing a pamphlet when there has been indicated the purpose for which she is preparing same? This is superficial! This has to be reached before there is begun any actuality of preparation, and followed with a purpose, with a desire. Such cannot be prepared for anyone! It has to be sought. Such data are prepared by those who give of themselves!

Did the Father prepare the Master, or did the Master prepare Himself for the Father's purpose?

Then would [2067] prepare herself for that she hopes to give to others, or would that to be given prepare [2067]?

(Q) Why do historians like Josephus ignore the massacre of the infants, and the history of Christ, when they record minute details of all other historical events?

(A) What was the purpose of Josephus' writing? For the Jews or for the Christians? This answers itself! [**My note:** This question is covered further in the next chapter.]

(Q) In one Reading we are told Jesus' birthday was on March 19 according as we would reckon time now. In another Reading we were told that we keep Christmas about the right time, the 24th or 25th of December as we have our time now. Please explain seeming contradiction.

(A) Both are correct according to the time from which same were reckoned. How many times have there been the reckonings? Take these in consideration, with the period of events being followed in the information indicated. Just as there was the reckoning from the various groups for their individual activity, so was the information given as to the records from that source with which those seeking were concerned.

[**My note:** As we will learn in the next chapter, the date for the birth of Jesus is off a bit. It has been determined by dating Herod's decree to kill all baby boys under the age of two in an effort to kill baby Jesus, and that decree occurred around 6 BCE, and if we combined this with an astronomical event so brilliant in the sky that it may have been the so-called "Star of Bethlehem" that occurred February through March in 6 BCE when the planets Jupiter, Saturn, and Mars formed a bright triangle in the sky above, we have a likely date. Now this still does not explain Cayce's answer, but it's something to consider.]

(Q) A Reading states that the historic events from the time of the prophets until Christ were written by Thesea, Herod's wife. [See 2067-1, Par. 57 indicating her writings were *based on* the Alexandrian and the "city in hills" records.] Why did her children destroy these writings in the Alexandrian Library, and are there any of these writings left on earth at the present time?

(A) Her children did not destroy them. They were destroyed by the Mohammedans and the divisions in the church, who were of the Jews and not the Romans nor the mixture of the Roman and Jewish influence. There are not those records save as may be attained from some present in the Vatican.

(Q) Was Jesus as a child also able to perform miracles, as the Catholic Church claims, and was he clairaudient, clairvoyant, and did He remember His past incarnations?

(A) Read the first chapter of John and you will see. As to the activities of the child—the apparel brought more and more the influence which today would be called a lucky charm, or a lucky chance; not as a consciousness. This began (the consciousness) with the ministry from that period when He sought the activities from the entrance into the temple and disputing or conversing with the rabbi at the age of twelve. Thus the seeking for the study through the associations with the teachers at that period.

(Q) Is it true that Jesus in His youth loved Mary, Martha's sister as a sweetheart, or did He never have a sweetheart?

(A) Mary, the sister of Martha, was an harlot—until the cleansing; and not one that Jesus would have loved, though He loved all. The closer associations brought to the physical or filial love, were with the children—and not with those the age of the Master.

(Q) Please give facts about Jesus' education in Palestine, the schools He attended, how long, what He studied, and under what name He was registered.

(A) The periods of study in Palestine were only at the time of His sojourn in the temple, or in Jerusalem during those periods when He was quoted by Luke as being among the rabbi or teachers. His studies in Persia, India, and Egypt covered much greater periods. He was always registered under the name Jeshua.

(Q) Please describe Jesus' education in India, schools attended—did He attend the Essene school in Jagannath taught by Lamaas, and did He study in Benares also under the Hindu teacher Udraka?

(A) He was there at least three years. Arcahia was the teacher.

(Q) Did He attend the schools in Jagannath-

(A) *All* were a portion of the teachings as combined from the Essene schools, but these were not the true Essene doctrine as practiced by the Jewish and semi-Jewish associations in Carmel.

(Q) Did He study in Benares also under the Hindu teacher Udraka?

(A) Rather that as indicated—Arcahia.

(Q) Please describe Jesus' education in Egypt in Essene schools of Alexandria and Heliopolis, naming some of His outstanding teachers and subjects studied.

(A) Not in Alexandria—rather in Heliopolis, for the period of attaining to the priesthood, or the taking of the examinations there—as did John [the Baptist]. One was in one class, one in the other.

(Q) Please describe Jesus' contact with schools in Persia, and did He at Persepolis establish a method of entering the Silence as well as demonstrating healing power?

(A) Rather that was a portion of the activity in the "city in the hills and the plains." [Persian incarnation as Zend]

[**My note:** Gladys' note here is referring to Cayce readings indicating that Zend was the father of Zoroaster, the founder of Zoroastrianism in ancient Persia ca. 500 BCE, and a subsequent training center was located during Jesus' time in Shushtar, the so-called "city in the hills and the plains."]

(Q) Name some of His outstanding teachers and subjects studied.

(A) Not as teachers, but as being *examined* by these; passing the tests there. These, as they have been since their establishing, were tests through which ones attained to that place of being accepted or rejected by the influences of the mystics as well as of the various groups or schools in other lands. For, as indicated oft through this channel, the unifying of the teachings of many lands was brought together in Egypt; for that was the center from which there was to be the radial activity of influence in the earth—as indicated by the first establishing of those tests, or the recording of time as it has been, was and is to be—until the new cycle is begun.

(Q) Why does not the Bible tell of Jesus' education, or are there manuscripts now on earth that will give these missing details to be found soon?

(A) There are some that have been forged manuscripts. All of those that existed were destroyed—that is, the originals—with the activities in Alexandria. [**My note:** This is referring to the final burning of the Great Library in ancient Alexandria during the Muslim conquest of Egypt in 642 CE.]

(Q) Did Lazarus visit other planets and spiritual realms the four days his body lay in the tomb before Jesus raised him? [**My note:** This strange question is because Cayce taught that souls experience other dimensions while "dead" to earth life.]

(A) We haven't Lazarus here today! [**My note:** Occasionally Cayce did not have before his mind or mind's eye the information requested.]

(Q) Can you tell of angels, and visions, and dreams that strengthened Jesus, other than those mentioned in the Bible?

(A) If there will be recorded those signified by the periods of separation as indicated there, we will have sufficient for verification of this strengthening throughout His whole ministry. For, these occur at regular periods. [**My note:** I really can't help us better understand this answer.]

(Q) When did the knowledge come to Jesus that he was to be the Savior of the world?

(A) When he fell in Eden.

[**My note:** This strange reply is because Cayce's readings taught that the soul and spirit that was Jesus of Nazareth had many experiences prior to this most important incarnation. And he and many other souls were involved with the activities in the Garden of Eden. From Cayce's perspective, Adam was not only a person but a *soul group*. All of whom made the mistake called "original sin."]

(Q) Can you give the name of the lad who furnished the five loaves and two fishes at the feeding of the 5,000!

(A) We may supply same, but not from here.

(Q) What publisher would be likely to take a book of excerpts of Cayce Readings entitled Bible Characters Now Living? Is this writing advised?

(A) Not advised at present. Revell would supply the publication of such. [Fleming H. Revell Co.?]

(Q) Did Jesus study under Apollo and other Greek philosophers, and was it through educational contacts that the Greeks later came to Him to beg Him to come to their country when the Jews cast Him out?

(A) We do not find such. Jesus, as Jesus, never appealed to the worldly-wise.

(Q) Please explain more about Mary being the twin soul of Jesus and her refusal to reincarnate, and her deity?

(A) We do not find such as even being true.

[**My note:** This question is asked because there is a belief that Mary the mother of Jesus only appears in the form of *apparitions* (ghostly) and does not reincarnate. Also, other Cayce readings teach that Mary is the feminine portion or *yin* of the whole soul of which Jesus is the masculine portion or *yang*. I believe Cayce's answer to this question is because it was asked confusingly.]

(Q) In one Reading we are told the Wise Men came from India, Egypt, and Gobi; in another Reading we are told the Wise Man who brought the incense came from Persia. Which is correct, and besides the Wise Men Achlar and Ashtueil, what were the names of the other two Wise Men?

(A) Both are correct. There was more than one visit of the Wise Men. One is a record of three Wise Men. There was the fourth, as well as the fifth, and then the second group. They came from Persia, India, Egypt, and also from Chaldea, Gobi, and what is *now* the Indo or Tao land.

(Q) A Reading gives Sylvia as a man stoned with Stephen, and Anniaus as a woman of the household of Cyrenus—are these names correct?

(A) Correct.

(Q) Teleman, in a Reading, was reported as being of household where Philemon was a servant—is that the same Philemon whose servant Paul sent back?

(A) Same Philemon.

(Q) Was Judas Iscariot's idea in betraying Jesus to force Him to assert Himself as a King and bring in His kingdom then?

(A) Rather the desire of the man to force same, and the fulfilling of that as Jesus spoke of same at the supper.

[**My note:** The context of this comment by Cayce is from the Bible passage in Mark 14:10–21: "Judas Iscariot, who was one of the twelve, went to the chief priests in order to betray him to them. And when they heard it they were glad, and promised to give him money. And he sought an opportunity to betray him. And on the first day of Unleavened Bread, when they sacrificed the passover lamb, his disciples said to him, 'Where will you have us go and prepare for you to eat the passover?' And he sent two of his disciples, and said to them, 'Go into the city, and a man carrying a jar of water will meet you; follow him and wherever he enters, say to the householder, "The Teacher says, Where is my guest room, where I am to eat the passover with my disciples?" And he will show you a large upper room furnished and ready; there prepare for us.' And the disciples set out and went to the city, and found it as he had told them; and they prepared the passover. And when it was evening he came with the twelve. And as they were at table eating, Jesus said, 'Truly, I say to you, one of you will betray me, one who is eating with me.' They began to be sorrowful, and to say to him one after another, 'Is it I?' He said to them, 'It is one of the twelve, one who is dipping bread into the dish with me. For the Son of man goes as it is written of him, but woe to that man by whom the Son of man is betrayed! It would have been better for that man if he had not been born.'"

And this is the Old Testament prophecy that Jesus had been taught by his Essene teachers to which Cayce is referring, it is a line in Psalm 41 foreshadowing the betrayal: "Even my bosom friend in whom I trusted, who ate of my bread, has lifted his heel against me." (Psalm 41:9 or 10 depending upon which translation you're reading) Another is found in Zechariah 11:4-17, in which the prophet speaks of thirty pieces of silver and of a good shepherd, whose service is brought to an end by this betrayal. As explained in Matthew 26:15, Judas was paid thirty silver coins for his betrayal of Jesus. Judas told the authorities when and where they could arrest Jesus without being surrounded by a large crowd of Jesus' followers. As explained in Matthew 27:5–7, Judas later tossed the money into the Temple ("the house of the Lord") and the money was used to buy a potter's field (land so full of clay that it is no good for crops but potters use it to get clay for their pottery) as a burial place for foreigners (potter's fields were used for mass, unmarked graves of paupers and strangers). Here's a passage in Zechariah 11:12–13 that is amazingly prophetic: "I told them, 'If you think it best, give me my pay; but if not, keep it.' So they paid me thirty pieces of silver. And the Lord said to me, 'Throw it to the potter' – the handsome price at which they priced me! So I took the thirty pieces of silver and threw them into the house of the Lord to the potter." This passage is estimated to have been written in roughly 630 BCE, long before Mary gave birth to Jesus. Yet, Jesus was taught this prophecy and how it would be fulfilled by him in his present lifetime, as Jesus stated in Mark 14:21, "The Son of man goes as it is written of him."

Now here is a startling Q & A in Cayce's readings about the *reincarnation* of Judas Iscariot:

(Q) Is [5770] Judas Iscariot?

(A) 'Judas Iscariot, betrayer of me.' [Is this Jesus answering?]

(Q) He is a fine man today.

(A) A fine man and leans upon you. Many have been the trials of this soul in the destruction of many places and cities. Yet, though today with much of what the world calls material bounty, he leans upon you—yet, this soul leans on you.

(Q) Should he be introduced into the work at Virginia Beach?

(A) Yes, the more that are gathered in His name, the greater is the strength thereof. (137-125)

When I first read this my whole mind seemed to freeze momentarily, it was so surprising and fascinating. I truly felt "If Judas can redeem himself, then surely anyone can redeem himself."

Now let's go on with the reading we were reading, 2067–7:

(Q) Is Herod the Great now on earth, and will he be located through the Readings?

(A) We haven't Herod the Great.

(Q) Was Mary and Elizabeth taught in a sacred grove in Egypt for a time by teachers, Elihu and Salome, that they might better instruct their sons, Jesus and John?

(A) We do not find this to be true. Their education was rather with those headed by the Essenes through which Zachariah [father of John the Baptist] was called as the one to and through whom would come those influences as became the forerunner of the Christ. These were rather in the Palestine land. They were in the Holy Land, and at Mount Moriah. [**My note:** Mount Moriah is the name of the elongated north-south stretch of land lying between Kidron Valley and "Hagai" Valley, which runs between Mount Zion to the west and the Mount of Olives to the east. It is the mount upon which the High Priest Melchizedek blessed Abram (later Abraham) with bread and wine, the mount where Abraham was going to sacrifice Isaac, the mount where Jacob had his dream of the stairway to and from heaven, where David placed the Holy of Holies, and some believe it is where Solomon built the Great Temple, and where the Dome of the Rock stands today. It is considered by some to be the "navel of world." Some scholars disagree, identifying this mount with Mount Gerizim, where Jesus met "the Samaritan woman at the well."]

(Q) Please describe Jesus' initiations in Egypt, telling if the Gospel reference to "three days and nights in the grave or tomb," possibly in the shape of a cross, indicate a special initiation. [**My note:** Some believe this initiation occurred inside the sarcophagus in the King's Chamber of the Great Pyramid in Giza.]

(A) This is a portion of the initiation—it is a part of the passage through that to which each soul is to attain in its development, as has the world through each period of their incarnation in the earth. As is supposed, the record of the earth through the passage through the tomb, or the pyramid, is that through which each entity, each soul, as an initiate must pass for the attaining to the releasing of same—as indicated by the empty tomb, which has *never* been filled, see? Only Jesus was able to break same, as it became that which indicated His fulfillment.

[**My note:** The sarcophagus in the King's Chamber has a large chunk of its pink granite missing. And no mummy was ever found inside it, it was empty when first discovered.]

And there, as the initiate, He went out—for the passing through the initiation, by fulfilling—as indicated in the baptism in the Jordan; not standing in it and being poured or sprinkled either! as He passed from that activity into the wilderness to meet that which had been His undoing in the beginning.

[**My note:** This statement is referring to Cayce's teaching in reading 2067-7 that the soul we know as Jesus of Nazareth had previous incarnations, one of which was as Adam in the Garden of Eden, when he experienced original sin: "(Q) When did the knowledge come to Jesus that he was to be the Savior of the world? (A) When he fell in Eden." After his baptism and the Holy Spirit's descent upon him, he went into the desert to face three tests by Satan. These tests were associated with his initial fall from grace in the Garden as Adam. Of course, he now passed the tests and is ready to redeem all souls who carry the curse of original sin.]

We are through for the present.
Copy to Self, Ass'n file

Original sin is based on a belief that ancestors transmit to their heirs hereditary diseases. Christian doctrine extends this, believing that humanity's state of sin resulted from the original fall of humanity, stemming from Adam's and Eve's rebellion in Eden. Now all humanity has been "poisoned" or "infected" by the fruit from the Tree of the Knowledge of Good *and Evil.*

This next reading was for a female Persian spiritual leader who often visited Judy and others in Palestine during the preparations and birth of Jesus Christ. Besides its historical information, it reveals how Cayce is guiding us to become more universal in our thinking and acting and less individual, not so personal but more a channel of the Divine influence flowing through us—through our thinking and interacting with others.

TEXT OF READING 2880-2
F 56

This Psychic Reading given by Edgar Cayce at the office of the Association, Arctic Crescent, Virginia Beach, Va., this 22nd day of March, 1943, in accordance with request made by the self Mrs. [2880], Associate Member of the Ass'n for Research & Enlightenment, Inc.

PRESENT

Edgar Cayce; Gertrude Cayce, Conductor; Gladys Davis, Steno.

READING

Time of Reading 10:40 to 11:15 A. M. Eastern War Time. . . . , N.Y.

GC: You will have before you the entity now known as [2880], born July 23rd, 1886, at Liverpool, England, who seeks detailed information concerning her Palestine sojourn as Zermada at the time [1472] was leader of the Essenes, covering the entity's entire life, work, and associations throughout that experience from her entrance to her departure. You will also give the developing or retarding associations and influences of that incarnation which bear on her present life, activities, and associations, and how they may be best used in the entity's present experience for her individual development and greatest service to others. You will then answer the questions she will submit as they are asked.

EC: Yes—we are given the records here of that entity now known as or called, [2880], and the experiences of the entity in that period high-lighted by the associations of the entity with the Essenes and the leader in Palestine of that particular group.

As indicated, the entity now called [2880]—then Zermada—was rather of the Syrophenician, or the Persian and the Syrophenician peoples—as they were known in that experience. **[My note:** A Syrophenician is a Gentile born in the Phoenician part of Syria, as in syro-phoenician. Jesus healed the daughter of a Syrophenician in Mark 7:25-29: "Now the woman was a Greek, a Syrophoenician by birth. And she begged him to cast the demon out of her daughter. And he said to her, 'Let the children [of Israel] first be fed, for it is not right to take the children's bread and throw it to the dogs.' But she answered him, 'Yes, Lord; yet even the dogs under the table eat the children's crumbs.' And he said to her, 'For this saying you may go your way;

the demon has left your daughter.' And she went home, and found the child lying in bed, and the demon gone."]

In its unfoldment during the period the entity, as would be called now, took on the study of astrology, or astrological activities; growing in the early period in the experiences as a dreamer, as a meditator, as a seeress or prophetess; making those associations with the peoples of then far east.

Coming early in its experience to the conclusions, from its own experiences, that the looked for changes were coming in the Holy or Promised Land, the entity—before the birth of the Christ-child—made many journeys, and finally there were the closer associations with the leader of the Essenes and the entity dwelt in Carmel.

Through those associations there came more communications and interpretations of those records or signs that eventually brought the journeys of some of the Wise Men, of which we have records. These were the high-lights of the entity's experiences through that particular period of activity.

As to the associations, many of those of other lands came to the entity, with the counseling together. The associations with Judy as the leader of the Essene peoples only intensified or made the preparations as to choosing the groups that were to be the channels through which there was the possibility, the probability that the awakening should come to the peoples of that period; as well as to the world.

There were many of those who were a part of the associations in those activities; some where there were disputations, some where there were agreements. And as indicated for the entity, in the application or use of the findings, studies or interpretations of the various combinations of astrological influences—the Persian manners of interpretation should be used. These would come to be more in keeping with those that were the unfoldments and developments of the entity through that particular period.

As to the developments or retardments in the experience—these are the same problems that the entity has in the present; the intenseness of the entity, the ability to give those interpretations not only through the findings of others but through the intuitive forces as related to the soul-development of the entity.

The individual problems with individuals through the experience—these, as then, have not as yet been concluded in their relationships.

For, this would bring questions, such as this: What is the purpose of an individual's entrance into the activities in the earth? That the soul may be a witness to the glorifying of the first cause or purpose, or God, in the earth. Whenever these have not been wholly attained, they continue to be problems in the individual entity's experience.

After the birth of the forerunner [John the Baptist], and the problems that such brought to the priests that had conformed to or become a part of the experience, the entity was not altogether a dweller in Carmel—or the Promised Land, for fear of those in political power as to the activities. This caused the entity to go back and forth a great deal [between Jerusalem and Carmel]. Much of these were secret meetings, or what would be called not open visitations. Yet the entity throughout its experience continued to be one to whom many in places came seeking information, for direction and counsel.

The entity lived to be nearly ninety years of age in that particular period, passing into the other consciousness in a period of journey coming toward the Carmel retreat.

Ready for questions.

(Q) Please give me the origin of the seal referred to in my Life Reading; an interpretation of its figures; its relationship to my activities both past and present; instructions for arranging the figures to form the symbol mentioned; how the symbolism can be constructively used so that its meaning can be recognized and applied, and tell me if it should be used as a motive for meditation?

(A) If the Life Reading is interpreted, it will be seen the activities in the experience are represented in the seal by the symbols. The interpretation is that these symbols should enable the entity to visualize the proper interpretation of problems in the lives of others. It is *not* as a motive for meditation, but the symbols are signs—just as given in the beginning, that the sun, the moon, the stars are given as signs, as symbols; and these should allow—in periods of meditation—the questions and answers to others, as well as enabling self to be made aware of—or given, we might say—the cue, or the key, or a prompting. Not to be used as a reason for meditation, rather as the answer in meditation.

(Q) What are the intents and purposes for which I came into this present experience as referred to in my Life Reading?

(A) Just as indicated, to *complete* the purposes in using each ability to the glory of the First Cause, or God—never as that of gratifying, satisfying of self alone, but as an enlightening influence, as a helpfulness, as an inspiration, as a guiding force to many.

(Q) How can I attain better integration and greater balance?

(A) Losing self in Him. Or, as would be put orthodoxly, "by faith." As may be put by reason, "studying to show self approved unto God, a workman not ashamed, but rightly stressing those things in the experience of all that are creative; minimizing faults, magnifying virtues."

(Q) Please give me a full account of the relationship and activities with my present son, [2850], during my incarnation as Zermada in Palestine, as well as other periods, explaining the cause of my present intense desire to protect him from harm or unhappiness, instructing me as to how I can be of the greatest service to him in the present?

(A) Only as may be indicated here in this experience may it be given here, for these are the records as we have. As indicated in the records of each in this particular period of activity—one—the son now—was rather intense, headstrong in his activities. The entity itself was rather inclined to temperate activity, and not too much of the urge to be so aggressive as the son was. Hence in the present we find those undue anxieties of the entity, knowing innately the intenseness to which this soul-entity, the son, would and does go in his seeking.

(Q) Please give me a detailed account of my association during my Palestine incarnation as Zermada, as well as during other life periods, with my present husband, [. . .], the purpose of our present relationship and how we may best further the development of each other now.

(A) These should be taken as a whole, if there is to be the perfect understanding. In that experience it was rather the passive period of activity, as it finds in the present; yet there were other associations which, as indicated, create or give the tensions. But the beauty, the rhythm, the symmetrical activity, comes from that particular period of sojourn. Hence the bond of sympathy, the bond of a united effort is the channel, the manner; not only in the material things but in the meditation and purpose, the hopeful purposes. These should be coordinated, that collaboration in the application of abilities of each in the present may be rather unified in their interpretation in material things.

(Q) Please give a fuller account of my association in Palestine with the entity now known as [1472 Judy]—then also called [1472 Judy]—and interpret the frequent vision in which I see us together on a high tower or battlement looking out over what seems to be a desert land, giving the significance of the fact that, in the vision, [1472], wears a headdress with her robe, while I wear a similar robe without a headdress?

(A) There's little more than that as given. They counseled together oft, but they each considered self as an authority in or among their particular group. Do not get the idea that there was whole consideration of either, but that each had her own inner groups to which the counsel meant much, when to others at that period it meant little. Yet there was kept ever that bond of sympathy, that bond of purposefulness between the two; for each realized in the experience the less of self—or as was aptly given by the forerunner, "He must increase and I decrease." Neither finds that in self in the present, but that must be the principle. In the interpretation of the Christ-Consciousness, it must increase while self is lost in the giving to others. Neither holds to this, but you will find it in the end.

As to the vision—this is an interpreting of experiences when individuals met in Carmel. The battlement was where the two entities met in their discussions of their findings, and for their choice as to which each is to give to her own particular group. The vision of the headdress merely represents the customs and the differences of the peoples or tribes or groups to which the two belonged.

(Q) Considering the statement in my Life Reading that my present son, [2850], my present husband, [. . .], and the entities now known as [1472] and [2795] were all closely associated with me during my Palestine incarnation as Zermada, please give the character of the relationship between each of us at that time, and its bearing on the present, especially that between [2850] and [1472] and [2850] and [2795].

(A) We haven't [2795] or [2850]. We are giving as to what *this* entity, [2880] may do! These are *their* problems! For this entity the problems then, as outlined, were the considerations given each for a general purpose or awakening for all, see? as a universal truth; not as an individual but as for a universal truth. This may be best illustrated in that just given. Thus the activities in the present of the entity as in relationship to each of the individuals named—Judy, the husband, the son, the friend—aid as a stimuli to each in that unfoldment of the knowledge, of the application of the consciousness of the power manifested in the Christ-Consciousness in the heart of each; magnifying the virtues, minimizing the faults of each, and as one to another; taking the broader view, not the individual characterization of same.

(Q) When, where, and what has been my association in former incarnations with the entity now known as Olga Worrell, and what is the purpose of our present friendship?

(A) We haven't Worrell.

We are through for the present.

Copy to Self, [1472], Ass'n file

This next reading is for the author of the most famous biography of Edgar Cayce, *There is a River*, written by Thomas Sugrue. Sugrue needs Cayce to answer some questions for him as he finishes the manuscript.

TEXT OF READING 5749-8

This psychic reading given by Edgar Cayce at his home on Arctic Crescent, Virginia Beach, Virginia, this 27th day of June, 1937, in accordance with request made by the self—Mr. Thomas Sugrue, Active Member of the Ass'n for Research & Enlightenment, Inc.

PRESENT

Edgar Cayce; Gertrude Cayce, Conductor; Gladys Davis, Steno. Thomas Sugrue and Hugh Lynn Cayce.

READING

Time of Reading 4:15 to 4:50 P. M.

GC: You will have before you the entity, Thomas Sugrue, present in this room. You will now continue with the information on the life and history of the Master, beginning now with detail information on the group which was preparing for the coming of the Christ, giving name of group, names of members who figured prominently in the active preparation; relating the signs, symbols and visions which indicated to this group that the time was at hand. You will then answer the questions that may be asked:

EC: Yes, we have the entity here, Thomas Sugrue, with the desire and the purpose for the understanding and knowledge of the physical experience of the Master's in the earth.

In those days when there had been more and more of the leaders of the peoples in Carmel—the original place where the school of prophets was established during Elijah's time, Samuel—these were called then Essenes; and those that were students of what ye would call astrology, numerology, phrenology [**My note:** From the Greek word *phren,* meaning "mind," and *logos,* meaning "knowledge," it is a pseudoscience primarily focused on measurements of the human skull, based on the concept that the brain is the organ of the mind, and that certain brain areas have localized, specific functions or modules.], and those phases of that study of the return of individuals—or incarnation.

These were then the reasons that there had been a proclaiming that certain periods were a cycle; and these had been the studies then of Arestole [384-322 BCE, a Greek philosopher and scientist], Enos, Mathias, Judas, and those that were in the care or supervision of the school—as you would term.

These having been persecuted by those of the leaders, this first caused that as ye have an interpretation of as the Sadducees, or "There is no resurrection," or there is no incarnation, which is what it meant in those periods. [**My note:** Here Cayce is explaining that in those days the term "resurrection" meant *incarnate* life after death, thus *reincarnation.* The ancient Egyptians mummified their bodies and the bodies of their animals in a belief that they could animate them again, or resurrect them. The soul lives again in the flesh.]

In the lead of these, with those changes that had been as the promptings from the positions of the stars—that stand as it were in the dividing of the ways between the universal, that is the common vision of the solar system of the sun, and those from without the spheres—or as the common name, the North Star, as its variation made for those cycles that would be incoordinant with those changes that had been determined by some—this began the preparation—for the three hundred years, as has been given, in this period. [**My note:** Cayce's readings teach that changes can be seen in the cycles of celestial movements and earth's shifts in its poles and magnetic fields. And it has been determined that the Pole Star or North Star of the earth has changed and will change again. In ancient times the star Thuban in the constellation of Draco was the pole star, now Polaris in Ursa Minor (the Little Dipper), and eventually Vega in Lyra constellation.]

Those in charge at the time were Mathias, Enos, Judas.

In these signs then was the new cycle, that as was then—as we have in the astrological—the beginning of the Piscean age, or that position of the Polar Star or North Star as related to the southern clouds. These made for the signs, these made for the symbols; as would be the sign as used, the manner of the sign's approach and the like.

These then were the beginnings, and these were those that were made a part of the studies during that period.

Then there were again those soundings—that is, the approach of that which had been handed down and had been the experiences from the sages of old—that an angel was to speak. As this occurred when there was the choosing of the mate that had—as in only the thought of those so close—been immaculately conceived, these brought to the focal point the preparation of the mother.

Then when there were those periods when there was the dumbness to the priest and he, Zacharias, was slain for his repeating of same in the hearing of those of his own school, these made for those fears that made the necessary preparations for the wedding, the preparations for the birth, the preparations for those activities for the preservation (physically) of the child; or the flight into Egypt. [**My note:** In this context Zacharias (phonetic spelling) is the same person as Zechariah, the father of John the Baptist. He was made dumb by the angel who told him of his coming son (Luke 1:20) but later regained his voice when the boy was born and he loudly declared as the angel had instructed, for which he was subsequently murdered by his colleagues.]

Ready for questions.

(Q) Is the teaching of the Roman Catholic Church that Mary was without original sin from the moment of her conception in the womb of Ann, correct?

(A) It would be correct in *any* case. Correct more in this. For, as for the material teachings of that just referred to, you see: In the beginning Mary was the twin-soul of the Master in the entrance into the earth! [**My note:** Cayce teachings that all souls have masculine and feminine qualities in oneness, the yang and yin. When God separated the genders in Genesis 2:18-15 these qualities began a journey of separate expression in specific masculine and feminine bodies. Thus, the Logos, the Messiah, the Christ is expressed in the earth in both a masculine form and a feminine form, Adam in one and Eve in the other. And these two expressions have incarnated together many times in order to keep the Light on in the earth among all the souls. From Cayce's view, Mary is the incarnation of the feminine portion of the Logos, Messiah, and Christ, while Jesus is the masculine. They are "twin-souls" or the twins of the *one* original soul that God created in Genesis 1 and placed in the Garden of Eden in Genesis 2.]

(Q) Was Ann prepared for her part in the drama as mother of Mary?

(A) Only as in the general, not as specific as Mary after Mary being pointed out.

See, there was no belief in the fact that Ann proclaimed that the child was without father. It's like many proclaiming today that the Master was immaculately conceived; they say "Impossible!" They say that it isn't in compliance with the natural law. It *is* a natural law, as has been indicated by the projection of mind into matter and thus making of itself a separation to become encased in same—as man did.

Then, that there has been an encasement was a beginning. Then there must be an end when this must be or may be broken; and this began at that particular period. Not the only—this particular period with Ann and then the Master *as* the son; but the *only* begotten of the Father in the flesh *as* a son *of* an immaculately conceived daughter!

(Q) Neither Mary nor Jesus, then, had a human father?

(A) Neither Mary nor Jesus had a human father. They were one *soul* so far as the earth is concerned; because [else] she would not be incarnated in flesh, you see. [**My note:** Here Cayce is indicating that Mary's soul was so divine that she wouldn't even be expressed in the flesh or physicality without the "Most High" (Hebrew *El-yon*) conceiving her to be so. Read how the angel speaks to her in Luke 1:28-38 and you'll see how special she is.]

(Q) How were the maidens selected and by whom?

(A) By all of those who chose to give those that were perfect in body and in mind for the service; and as Ann—or Anna—gave the same, and in the presentation could not be refused because of the perfectness of body, though many questioned and produced a division because she proclaimed it had been conceived without knowing a man.

Thus came the division, yet the others were chosen—each as a representative of the twelve [**My note:** This is referring to the twelve holy girls not the twelve apostles.] in the various phases that had been or that had made up Israel—or man.

(Q) How old was Mary at the time she was chosen?

(A) Four; and, as ye would call, between twelve and thirteen when designated as the one chosen by the angel on the stair.

(Q) Describe the training and preparation of the group of maidens.

(A) Trained as to physical exercise first, trained as to mental exercises as related to chastity, purity, love, patience, endurance. All of these by what would be termed by many in the present as persecutions, but as tests for physical and mental strength; and this under the supervision of those that cared for the nourishments by the protection in the food values. These were the manners and the way they were trained, directed, protected.

(Q) Were they put on special diet?

(A) No wine, no fermented drink ever given. Special foods, yes. These were kept balanced according to that which had been first set by Aran [**My note:** Aaron? See Leviticus 10:9 and 11:1-47] and Ra Ta.

(Q) In what manner was Joseph informed of his part in the birth of Jesus?

(A) First by Mathias or Judah. Then as this did not coincide with his own feelings, first in a dream and then the direct voice.

And whenever the voice, this always is accompanied with odors as well as lights; and oft the description of the lights is the vision, see?

(Q) Why was he disturbed when Mary became with child while yet a virgin?

(A) Owing to his natural surroundings and because of his advanced age to that of the virgin when she was given; or as would be termed in the present, because of what people say. Yet when assured, you see, that this was the divine, not only by his brethren but by the voice and by those experiences, he knew. For you see there was from the time of the first promise, while she was still yet in training from the choice, there was a period of some three to four years; yet when he went to claim her as the bride, at the period of—or between sixteen and seventeen, she was found with child.

(Q) How old was Joseph at the time of the marriage?

(A) Thirty-six.

(Q) How old was Mary at the time of the marriage?

(A) Sixteen.

(Q) At what time after the birth of Jesus did Mary and Joseph take up the normal life of a married couple, and bring forth the issue called James?

(A) Ten years. Then they came in succession; James, the daughter, Jude.

[**My note:** The daughter's name was Ruth. There is a passage in the New Testament that indicates that Jesus had brothers and that they were asking for Jesus: "While he [Jesus] was still speaking to the people, behold, his mother and his brothers stood outside, asking to speak to him." Matthew 12:46]

(Q) Give a detailed description for literary purposes, of the choosing of Mary on the temple steps.

(A) The temple steps—or those that led to the altar, these were called the temple steps. These were those upon which the sun shone as it arose of a morning when there were the first periods of the chosen maidens going to the altar for prayer; as well as for the burning of the incense.

On this day, as they mounted the steps all were bathed in the morning sun; which not only made a beautiful picture but clothed all as in purple and gold.

As Mary reached the top step, then, then there were the thunder and lightning, and the angel led the way, taking the child by the hand before the altar. This was the manner of choice, this was the showing of the way; for she led the others on *this* particular day.

(Q) Was this the orthodox Jewish temple or the Essene temple?

(A) The Essenes, to be sure.

Because of the adherence to those visions as proclaimed by Zacharias in the orthodox temple, he (Zacharias) was slain even with his hands upon the horns of the altar.

Hence these as were being here protected were in Carmel, while Zacharias was in the temple of Jerusalem.

(Q) Was Mary *required* to wait ten years before knowing Joseph?

(A) Only, you see, until Jesus went to be taught by others did the normal or natural associations come; not required—it was a choice of them both because of their *own* feelings.

But when He was from without the roof and under the protection of those who were the guides (that is, the priests), these associations began then as normal experiences.

(Q) Were the parents of John the messenger members of the band which prepared for Jesus?

(A) As has just been indicated, Zacharias at first was a member of what you would term the orthodox priesthood. Mary and Elizabeth were members of the Essenes, you see; and for this very reason Zacharias kept Elizabeth in the mountains and in the hills. Yet when there was the announcing of the birth and Zacharias proclaimed his belief, the murder, the death took place.

(Q) Where was the wedding performed? of Mary and Joseph?

(A) In the temple there at Carmel.

(Q) Where did the couple live during the pregnancy?

(A) Mary spent the most of the time in the hills of Judea, portion of the time with Joseph in Nazareth. From there they went to Bethlehem to be taxed, or to register—as ye would term.

(Q) Who assisted as midwife?

(A) This has been touched upon through these sources; and as the daughter of the Innkeeper and those about assisted and aided, these have seen the glory, much, in their experiences.

(Q) Do we celebrate Christmas at approximately the right time?

(A) Not a great variation, for there having been the many changes in the accounting of time, or accounting for the periods from the various times when time is counted—not far wrong—twenty-fourth, twenty-fifth of December, as ye have your time now.

(Q) Who were the parents of Joseph?

(A) That as recorded by Matthew, as is given, you see; one side recorded by Matthew, the other by Luke—these on various sides but of the house of David, as was also Mary of the house of David.

(Q) Were Mary and Joseph known to each other socially before the choosing for them to be man and wife?

(A) As would be chosen in a lodge, not as ye would term of visitations; neither as only chosen by the sect or the families. In those periods most of the Jewish families, the arrangements were made by the parents of the contracting parties, you see; while in this—these were not as contracting parties from their families. For Ann and her daughter were questioned as to belonging to any, you see! Then it was not a choice altogether as that they were appointed by the leaders of the sect or of the group or of the lodge or of the church; for this is the church that is called the Catholic now—and is the closest.

These were kept then in that way of choice between them, and choice as pointed out by the divine forces.

We are through for the present.

Copy to Self, Ass'n file

This next reading is about Edgar Cayce's incarnation during the Essene period in Palestine, being among the seventy disciples and then eventually becoming the Bishop of the "Church" of Laodicea. I put the word *church* in quotes because they were more like *assemblies* than formal churches of today, and they did not call them churches back then.

TEXT OF READING 294-192
M 60

This psychic reading given by Edgar Cayce at his home on Arctic Crescent, Virginia Beach, Va., this 11th day of February, 1938, in accordance with request made by the self.

PRESENT

Edgar Cayce; Gertrude Cayce, Conductor; Gladys Davis, Steno.

READING

Time of Reading 11:20 to 11:50 A. M. Eastern Standard Time . . . , Va.
(LIFE READING SUGGESTION for period as LUCIUS in PALESTINE.)

EC: Yes, we have the records of that entity now called Edgar Cayce; and those experiences in the earth's plane known as Lucius of Cyrene—or known in the early portion of the experience as Lucius Ceptulus, of Grecian and Roman parentage, and of the city of Cyrene.

[**My note:** ancient Greek and Roman city near present–day Shahhat, Libya. It was the oldest and most important of the five Greek cities in the region.]

As a developing youth and young man, Lucius was known rather as a ne'er-do-well; or one that wandered from pillar to post; or became—as would be termed in the present day parlance—a soldier of fortune.

When there were those activities in and about Jerusalem and Galilee of the ministry of the man Jesus, Lucius came into those environs.

Being impelled by the experiences with the followers, and the great lessons as given by the Teacher, he became rather as one that was a hanger-on, and of the very intent and purpose that this was to be the time when there was to be a rebellion against the Roman legions, the Romans in the authority.

And the entity Lucius looked forward to same; acting rather in the capacity of not an informant but rather as one attempting to keep in touch with the edicts of the various natures between the political forces in Rome and the political forces among the Jews.

The entity was disregarded and questioned by those who were of the Jewish faith who were the close followers of the Master; yet it was among those that were sent as those who were to be as teachers—or among the Seventy.

With the arousing, and the demanding that there be more and more of the closer association with the Teacher, Lucius being of the foreign group was rejected as one of the Apostles; yet was questioned mostly by John, Peter, Andrew, James, and those of the closer following—as Matthew, Bartholomew; and was the closer affiliated or associated with Thomas.

In those activities then that followed the Crucifixion, and the days of the Pentecost, and the sermon or teachings—and when there was beheld by Lucius the outpouring of the Holy Spirit, when Peter spoke in tongues—or as he spoke in his *own* tongue, it, the message was *heard* by those of *every* nation in their *own* tongue—this so impressed Lucius that there came a rededicating, and the determination within self to become the closer associated, the closer affiliated with the Disciples or Apostles.

But when the persecutions arose, and there was the choice of those that were to act as those called the deacons—as Philip and Stephen and the others—again he was rejected because of his close associations with one later called Paul, or Saul; he being also of Tarsus or of the country, and a Roman, and questioned as to his Jewish ancestry—though claimed by Paul (or Saul) that he was a Jew. His mother was indeed, and of the tribe of Benjamin, though his father was not. [**My note:** Saul was a native of Tarsus, the capital city of Cilicia, an early Roman province located on what is today the southern Mediterranean coast of Turkey.]

Hence we find the questions arose as to the advisability of putting those in position, either as teachers, ministers or those in active service, that were questioned as to their lineal descent.

And again the old question as to whether *any* were to receive the word but those of the household of faith, or of the Jews.

[**My note:** Peter was shocked when the Holy Spirit fell upon the Gentiles]

During the sojourn in Jerusalem, though, before the greater persecutions—that is, before the beheading of James the brother of John [**My note:** According to all four Gospels, Zebedee and his wife Salome were the parents of James the Lesser and John the Beloved, two apostles of Jesus. Zebedee lived at or near Bethsaida, the birthplace of three other apostles: Peter, Andrew, and Philip. Zebedee owned two fishing boats, so he was among the wealthier fishermen.], and the stoning of Stephen—here again we had a great question arise. For Lucius, through the associations with the one who became his companion or wife as ye would call, was entertained and kept by Mary and Martha and Lazarus—thus we find these again made questions.

And there is often the confusing of Lucius and Luke, for these were kinsmen; and Lucius and Luke were drawn or thrown together, and with the conversion of Saul (or Paul, as he became) they followed closer and closer with the activities of Paul."

Let's break here and view Cayce's reading number 1598-2 concerning who wrote the Gospels. Remember, when he raised his voice, his stenographer capitalized the words which are now italicized.

(Q) I am writing a book. Can you help me, from the hall of records? Who actually wrote the four Gospels? In what order? and when were they written?

(A) These as we find may *best* be determined by the investigations of the records as related to same; that is, to satisfy self as to its claim—or a physical record—in the Vatican's own libraries. These will be accessible, or made accessible, if there is the seeking, during this present year.

As we find, this will be the manner in which these are indicated; but *verify* same for self's *own* understanding, as well as self's satisfaction:

Mark was first dictated, greatly by Peter; and this in those periods just before Peter was carried to Rome. [**My note:** Where Peter was crucified in 44 CE. Interestingly, tradition holds that Mark wrote down the sermons of Peter, thus composing the Gospel according to Mark (Eusebius' *Ecclesiastical History,* 15–16), before Mark was exiled to Alexandria in 43 CE.]

The next was *Matthew,* written by the one whose name it bears—*as* for the *specific* reasons—to those who were scattered into the upper portions of Palestine and through Laodicea [**My note:** a region in Asia Minor, now modern-day Turkey]. This was written something like thirty-three to four years later than *Mark;* and while this body—that wrote same—was in exile [**My note:** to Alexandria, Egypt, where he was eventually martyred in 68 CE].

Luke was written by Lucius, rather than Luke; though a companion with Luke during those activities of Paul; and written, of course, unto those of the faith under the Roman *influence*—not to the Roman peoples but to the provinces ruled *by* the Romans! and it was from those sources that the very changes were made, as to the differences in that given by *Mark* and *Matthew.* [**My note:** There is no nativity scene in Mark as there is in Matthew, and

Matthew contains parables that are not in Mark. Matthew is 7,213 words longer than Mark, which is the shortest gospel.]

John was written by several; not by the John who was the beloved, but the John who *represented* or who was the scribe *for* John the beloved; and—as much of same—was written much later. Portions of it were written at different times and combined some fifty years after the Crucifixion." [88 CE?] (1598-2)

Now back to the reading we were studying, 294-192:

With the acceptance of Lucius by Paul, and part of those in the Caesarean church, Lucius determined—with his companion—to return to the portion of his own land, owing to the persecutions, and to their attempt to establish a church; to be the minister, to be the active force in those portions of the land. [**My note:** Lucius' original hometown was Cyrene, Libya, located in northern Africa. It was a Greek colony where 100,000 Judean Jews had been forced to settle during the reign of Alexander the Great's general Ptolemy Soter (323–285 BCE). But in this reading and in others (especially 2390-3) Cayce indicates that Lucius and his sister Nimmuo had a family home in Asia Minor at Laodicea. And it is here where Lucius and Nimmuo return during the Roman persecutions and became leaders of one of the Revelation's "Seven Churches of Asia Minor."]

Thus we find in those latter portions of the experience he became the bishop or the director or the president of the Presbytery; or what ye would call the priest or the father or the high counsellor as given to those in the early periods of the Church; that is, the one to whom *all questions* were taken respecting what ye would term in the present as theology, or questions pertaining to the laws.

In such the entity as the bishop was the last word, other than that there might be the appeal from such a verdict to the church in Jerusalem—or the Apostles themselves.

Such disputes brought disturbances at times, when there were the questionings especially as Paul brought into that region as to whether it was well for those in such positions to be married or not.

And the declarations as made through the Corinthian and the Ephesian leaders indicate what disturbances there were; because differences arose between Lucius and Paul as well as between Silas and Paul and Barnabas and those that had become the leaders or the real ministers or the missionaries for the Church.

Hence this brought into the experience of the entity Lucius disturbance between himself and his companion, because—in the first, the companion was younger in years than Lucius and to them there had been no offspring—no child.

This confusion made for periods when there was the withdrawing of the companion, and the closer association of the companion with the teacher that had been the proclaimer and the director in the early experience of the Master's life Himself—or with Judy [1472]; and with Elizabeth and with Mary the Mother of the Lord.

With those experiences, and with Paul's being carried on in his second and even his third missionary journey, and with *many* of the things propounded by him that Lucius had declared as things that were unstable, there again—with the teachings to the companion by Judy, by the Mother of the Lord and Elizabeth in their years of maturity teaching this younger person—was brought to Lucius that which later John proclaimed; that there *is* in this church of Laodicea no fault yet it is neither hot nor cold—and that for the lack of its very stand it would find condemning.

Those became periods when Lucius then was thrown the closer, or drawn the closer to the companion; and with the birth of the child there were brought those periods of the greater contentment and peace in the latter days of the entity called Lucius, and a seeing of the development of those experiences.

It may be questioned by some as to why such an *outstanding* experience of the entity now called Cayce should not have been given in the first.

As has been indicated, each entity, each individual *grows* or applies, or is meeting self in the varied experiences—as the tenets of an individual experience are applied in this present sojourn or activity.

If this had been given in the first, there would have been a puffing up—but the very unstableness as was indicated throughout the experience, until there were the lessons to be gained from the companion, may be seen.

Then meeting that companion in the present experience brings about that as may be given—that is the *humbleness* as was gained, *still* held.

Then these may become experiences in counseling, in giving to others what may become lessons—from questions of every nature that may arise from *every* phase of the human experience.

And indeed the entity as Lucius *in* the activities of the entity called Cayce may become an influence and a power for good in this present portion of this sojourn.

Ready for questions.

(Q) How closely was the entity associated with Andrew in that experience?

(A) Rather there was still questioning, for with Peter the speaker, Andrew the listener, there were disputes as to the advisability of Lucius being put into power; though in the latter portion of the experience we find—as has been indicated in Andrew's experience—they were rather close associated, and Andrew was a defender of Lucius—*after* there was the settling between the companion and Lucius, after their separation and then reuniting.

(Q) Please explain how all heard in their various tongues the message that was given by Peter in the one tongue. [**My note:** *glossolalia,* speaking in tongues, Acts 2:4]

(A) This was the activity of the spirit, and what the spirit indeed meant and means in the experiences of the individuals during that period.

For one that was of Cyrene heard a mixture of the Greek and Aryan tongue; while—though Peter spoke in the Arabic—those that were of the Hebrews heard in the Hebrew language; those in Greek heard in Greek, see? [**My note:** 9/22/39 See EC's explanation of this in letter to Mrs. [623] in 951-4 Background.]

We are through for the present.

Copy to Self " " Ass'n file

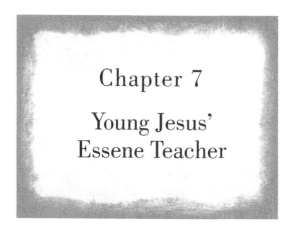

Chapter 7

Young Jesus' Essene Teacher

A mong the souls involved with the Essenes was an enlightened teacher, and this "he" was a *she!* Yes, despite the male dominance of those times the Essenes were taught and led by a woman—a woman who possessed mystical powers and a wide-reaching influence far beyond the borders of the Holy Land. And when Edgar Cayce was asked why she wasn't born a boy, he replied that this was "from the powers on high" and demonstrated *God's* view of woman's place in the affairs of humanity. It should be noted that Jesus included women in his entourage and his private small-group training. These women have often been referred to as "the holy women." Cayce attributed male dominance to man's misconception of woman's role in the fall in the Garden of Eden and what has been termed "original sin." Cayce also taught that a *soul* contains *both* yin and yang, or feminine and masculine qualities. And depth psychologist Carl Jung stated that one cannot be *fully* conscious if one is not in touch with the complementary gender dynamic *within* his subconscious. Jung termed the yin as *anima* and the yang as *animus*. According to Jung, a woman is expressing her femininity so her masculine qualities, or *animus*, would be in her deeper consciousness.

A man's *anima* would be in his deeper consciousness. For both women and men these complementary dynamics would appear when the outer person is subdued and the inner self is freer to express itself; thus in their *dreams* and *fantasies* the complement would appear. Male and female energetics will ultimately be one again when a person dies from this physical life and his/her soul departs, for the *soul* contains *both* in balance. In this world we express only one side of our whole soul, but in heaven we possess both, as Jesus taught: "In the resurrection they neither marry, nor are given in marriage, but are as angels in heaven." (Matthew 22:30) And though angels are mentioned in the Bible using a masculine pronoun, this is due to the limitations of the language, not an actual condition of angels. Angels do not have gender since gender is a biological function, and angels are not biological. Also, even the biblical term "Sons of God" includes females according to Cayce: "In the beginning there was presented that that became as the Sons of God, in that male and female were as one." (364-7) The Essenes were very much aware of this and considered women to be *equal* to men; they even had women priests and prophets, as stated in Luke 2:36–38 about Anna—of course this was only at the Essenes' temple on Mount Carmel, not at the main temple in Jerusalem: "There was a prophetess, Anna, the daughter of Phan'u-el, of the tribe of Asher; she was of a great age, having lived with her husband seven years from her virginity, and as a widow until she was eighty-four. She did not depart from the temple, worshiping with fasting and prayer night and day. And coming up at that very hour she gave thanks to God, and spoke of him [Jesus] to all who were looking for the redemption of Jerusalem."

In Cayce's reading of the "Book of Life" for the female Essene teacher, he said that she incarnated "in the spirit of Samson." (2067-11) This makes sense since in those challenging times she likely had to come with a strong spirit. And yet, Cayce gives this grand lady's name as simply "Judy." Curiously, her name in this recent incarnation with Edgar Cayce was Julia, but most everyone still called her Judy. Of course Judy is a diminutive of Judith (which is the feminine form of Judah, the fourth son of Jacob and Leah, and the founder of the Israelite of Tribe of Judah – in Revelation 5:5 we have, "Then one of the elders said to me, 'Do not weep! See, the Lion of the tribe of Judah, the Root of David, has triumphed. He is able to open the scroll and its seven seals.'"). The name Judith was given to another amazing women in Biblical history—one who has biblical book named after her. The Book of Judith is in the Bibles of the Roman Catholics and Eastern Orthodox Christians, while the Protestants and Hebrews placed this all-important book in their Apocrypha collection of spiritual books, but that still indicates their perceived value of this story. And consider what the famous Martin Luther—a professor of theology and groundbreaking figure in the Protestant Reformation—said about The Book of Judith: "If one could prove from established and reliable histories that the events in Judith really happened, it would be a noble and fine book, and should properly be in the Bible." Luther actually translated The Book of Judith and included it in the Appendix of his German Bible. The first-century Pope, St. Clement of Rome, held Judith to be an example of courageous love. Here's an excerpt from his Letter to the Corinthians, chapter 55: "Many women also, being strengthened by the grace of God, have performed numerous manly exploits. The blessed Judith, when her city was besieged, asked of the elders permission to go forth into the camp of the strangers; and, exposing herself to danger, she went out for the love which she bare to her country and people then besieged; and the Lord delivered Holofernes into the hands of a woman."

And St. Jerome describes Mary, the mother of Jesus, as a "new Judith" (*To Eustochium*: Letter 22, par. 21). Judith is also mentioned in the works of Dante (Paradiso Canto XXXII:1-36: "She is seated in Heaven, below the Virgin.") and Geoffrey Chaucer (The Merchant's Tale in *Canterbury Tales*, line 155: "Lo, Judith, as the ancient stories run, by her wise counsel she God's people kept, and Holofernes slew, while yet he slept . . . ").

Let me be clear, The Book of Judith was written some one hundred years *before* our Essene Judy and is *not* about her. However, this text gives us insight in Jewish tradition concerning women playing major roles in Israelite struggles against conquerors, and Judith was certainly one of the great ones. In a Samson-like act, Judith *decapitated* the commanding general of her enemy's army.

But she was not the only famous female liberator of the Israelites. These would include but are not limited to the following: Deborah (means "spirited or fiery woman" in Hebrew) who was the military leader who led her outnumbered and ill-equipped Israelite troops to a great victory. Jael (means "wild gazelle" in Hebrew) used a mallet to drive a tent stake into the head of the fearsome enemy general Sisera, who was fleeing Deborah's pursuit. Queen Esther (means "star" in Persian, her Hebrew name was *Hadassah*, derived from the fragrant and beautiful myrtle tree) helped free her people from Babylonian captivity and convinced her Persian king to fund and assist the rebuilding of Solomon's Temple that had been destroyed by the Babylonians. Queen Salome Alexandra of Jerusalem was a female *monarch* of Judea (141–67 BCE; her Hebrew name was *Shelamzion*, meaning "peace of Zion") and she is mentioned *twice* in the Essenes' *Dead Sea Scrolls!*

The Book of Judith is considered by most scholars to be *creative* history, mostly because it blends historical events with allegorical stories that are intended to inspire the heroic spirit of the Jewish people and assure that God is with them despite the mighty armies against them. The Book of Judith has two distinct parts of equal length. The first seven chapters describe the marching armies of King Nebuchadnezzar and his General Holofernes. These chapters describe military movements and periods of war interspersed with periods of calm and reflection. The seventh chapter ends as General Holofernes' warriors besiege the mountain-pass village of Bethulia, Judith's village. The next eight chapters tell of Judith, her prayers to God for help, and her self-sacrificing efforts to save her people. The final scenes reveal how she uses her ingenuity and womanly wiles to get invited into the general's tent, and when inside, during Holofernes' drunken stupor, she cuts his head off and takes it with her! Shocked and without their leader, Holofernes' army withdraws.

Cayce described our Essene Judy as "the feminine Samson" of her times (Samson literally means, "man of the sun"). Samson was a judge in Israel for some twenty years and a Nazarite (from *nazir*, meaning, "consecrated"), which is one who has taken an oath to serve God (Judges 13–16). A Nazarite took three vows: 1. abstain from wine, 2. refrain from cutting his hair, and 3. avoid contact with corpses and graves. Many of Judy's Essenes were also Nazarites. It should be noted that a Nazarene is not necessarily a Nazarite, but simply a person from Nazareth. Of course, a Nazarene could take a Nazarite vow if he chose. It should also be noted that "judges" in Israel were not overseers of the law or courts but *warriors* who handed out "justice" against Israel's enemies, usually by violent force. One should understand that Cayce's comparison of

Judy to Samson is not exactly a compliment, because Samson was a wildly destructive strongman who had many human flaws. He was not faithful to the Nazarite vows and could not establish any degree of domestic tranquility or companionship—not with a woman, a people, or even animals. Samson was a one-man war machine against the Philistines, killing many thousands barehanded or with nothing but a jawbone from a donkey for a weapon. Samson lived between 1118-1094 BCE during the Philistine rule over Israel. As a Nazarite, Samson's hair grew into long, black, curly locks, and his strength came from his hair, or more correctly, from the power it represented in his Nazarite agreement with God. When cut, God's power left him. It should be noted that the Nazarite vow was *put upon* Samson by his parents. They received the instruction to do this from an "Angel of the Lord." Samson did *not* choose the vow but was born into it. He certainly did not live up to the vow because he participated in wine-drinking parties and on one occasion he touched the corpse of a dead lion—both forbidden for a Nazarite. However, he appears to have taken the vow seriously in the latter part of his life, for when his hair that Delilah had cut off grew back, he implored God to give him his strength again so that he might strike at Israel's enemies one last time. Many scholars point out that Samson was the *vanguard* of the final overthrow of Philistine rule over Israel, followed by the efforts of Kings Saul and David, resulting in Solomon's reign of freedom: "Solomon ruled over all the kingdoms from the Euphrates to the land of the Philistines and to the border of Egypt. They brought tribute and served Solomon all the days of his life." (1 Kings 4:21, ca. 970 to 931 BCE)

One could assume that Cayce was indicating that Judy was a powerful leader of the Essenes and ruled with the energy and willpower of Samson. Even so, there is no indication that she had taken the Nazarite vow or killed Romans, as Samson killed Philistines. However, there were Zealots in her days, and these were sworn assassins of Romans. The Bible clearly indicates that Jesus knew these Zealots, and it is likely that Judy did. But neither Jesus nor Judy encouraged their murderous actions, despite what many perceived as justifiable killings.

Unlike Samson, Judy was definitely not a "Judge of *all* Israel" because, following the conquest of the northern kingdom of Israel by the Assyrians in 721 BCE, the ten tribes in that region disappeared from

history, now referred to as the "Lost Tribes of Israel." These tribes either
fled during the invasions and were exiled or were gradually assimilated
by the conquering people. The two remaining tribes in the southern
kingdom founded by Judah and Benjamin composed the Kingdom of
Judah, along with the priestly Levites. But this would not have been
during Judy's time. During her time there were the Sadducees (conser-
vatives who followed Moses' law to the letter, *see* Luke 20:27), Pharisees
(landowners and traders with pretensions to superior sanctity), Scribes
(lawyers—every village had to have at least one Jewish scribe), and
Samaritans (people initially brought from Babylon but eventually
abandoned their old idolatry and adopted portions of the Jewish religion (the "woman at the well" was among these, *see* the Gospel of John,
chapter 4); and, finally, Judy's group of Jewish Essenes. Among most
of the Jews of Judy's day, there was a feeling that God had abandoned
them and God's promises would not be unfulfilled, because the people
had failed in their part of covenant with God. But in the midst of all of
this despair there were those who still believed in the coming of the
Messiah as prophesied by the archangel Gabriel in the Book of Daniel,
some five-hundred years prior to Judy's time. Add to this that there
had not been a noteworthy, God-guided prophet in Israel for nearly
four-hundred years and we get a sense of the depth of despair among
the people now under Roman rule. However, among the Essenes, the
Messianic prophecy was alive and well. Essenes at Mount Carmel where
actually *looking* for that special female who would conceive and birth
the coming Messiah, as we learned in chapter 6.

In the Holy Land in the days of Judy's Essenes, Messianic hopes were
struggling to survive in the midst of Greco-Roman imperialism. Enslav-
ing conquered populations was common, and slaves made up a sizable
proportion of the population. The region had an assortment of ethnic
peoples with exotic religions. There was forced taxation. Greco-Roman
dress was the fashion. Baths, theaters, amphitheaters, hippodromes,
fountains, aqueducts, and arches were a part of life. With the Greco-Roman empires came safe travel which had never been possible before,
but with safe travel came the spread of disease. Physicians and healers
of all sorts were in great demand. Despite military control, murder and
mayhem were common in those days. Debauchery was also the norm
among the pagans. All of these facts cast a dark cloud over any lingering

hopes of the Messiah's coming.

As with the Philistines in Samson's time, Judy's people were under the rule of the materialistic and violent Romans who had little respect for the faith and pious practices of those they conquered. The Romans put in power local secular authorities, such as Herod the Great, who was an Arab (not a Moslem—that doesn't occur until 610 CE; we're in the late years of BCE, early years of CE). Herod was neither born of Jews nor raised in the Jewish faith and practices, but he pretended to be a Jew, even built a second temple in 18 BCE, known as the "Herod Temple." Upon his death in 4 BCE, the Romans divided his kingdom among three of his sons—Archelaus who oversaw Judea, Herod Antipas who oversaw Galilee and Peraea (eastern side of the Jordan River valley), and Philip who oversaw territories east of the Sea of Galilee.

You may be wondering how Herod could issue an edict to kill "all the male children who were in Bethlehem and all its vicinity, from two years old and under" (Matthew 2:16) in an effort to kill the baby Jesus whom the Magi had warned Herod would become the "King of the Jews." Well, most scholars now agree that Jesus' birth was most likely two or more years *earlier* than our present calendar would indicate. Scholars generally date Jesus' birth between 6 and 4 BCE. And we may also wonder how this horrific murdering of young children was not recorded in anyone's historical records, for it is not found in any documents of those times, only in the Bible. In his article, "Is the Account of the Slaughter of the Innocents Historical?" James Patrick Holding writes: "How many boys aged two and under could there have been in and around the tiny city of Bethlehem? Five? Ten? The Gospel of Matthew does not give a number. Professor William F. Albright, the dean of American archaeology in the Holy Land calculated the whole population of Bethlehem to have been roughly 300." But according to Cayce's readings and some other researchers, Mary and Joseph would likely have returned to Nazareth when Herod issued his murderous edict. The population of Nazareth has been estimated to have been around four hundred at that time. Cayce actually gave a reading for woman in Nazareth (308-3) whose baby boy was taken from her arms and killed before her eyes due to Herod's order. This surely indicates that Herod's order covered a broader area than one town, and this would have raised the number of baby boys murdered (Bethlehem and

Nazareth are some seventy miles apart.) Josephus, the Jewish historian of that time, in his *Antiquity of the Jews*, tells us that there were so many atrocities committed by Herod that he (Josephus) could not mention them all in his histories. But Josephus does tell us that Herod murdered a vast number of people and was so cruel to prisoners that they considered the dead to be lucky. Therefore, authorizing the killing of a few baby boys in "the little town of Bethlehem" and surrounding towns was a minor event in the bloody reign of Herod the Great, who even killed many of his own relatives.

According to Edgar Cayce's readings, Essene Judy served in many impressive roles:

She was the formal leader of the Essenes;

She was the principle teacher at the Essenes' temple on Mount Carmel;

She was a healer and prophetess;

She was one of the primary contacts for the star-guided Magi who came from the East to see the prophesied baby and better understand the meaning of his nativity;

And perhaps her greatest role: she was the teacher of young Jesus, particularly when he was between twelve and sixteen years old. And it was she who reconnected Jesus with the Magi when he became of age and arranged for him to go with the Magi to study in the East.

Like Samson, Judy had extraordinary abilities. Samson's powers were a combination of truly superhuman strength and fearlessness. For example, in one day Samson killed one thousand Philistine soldiers, not just men but *trained soldiers*, with nothing but a jawbone: "With the jawbone of an ass I have piled them in a mass, heaps upon heaps!" (Judges 15:16) But as amazing as Samson's powers were, Judy's powers were *supernatural!* Cayce said, "Judy's experience at that time was such that she might be present in many places without the physical body being there!" (2067-11) Cayce's reading states that she and Jesus could have conversations during his ministry wherever he was and while she remained physically at the temple on Mount Carmel because she could miraculously locate herself in two distinct places at the same time. (2067-11)

When Cayce was asked to describe what Judy taught young Jesus, he replied that Judy instructed the boy Jesus *in her home* about the *prophecies* pertaining to the mission of the Messiah and the *preordained* experiences that the promised Messiah would suffer. Surely at the top of this list would have been Psalm 22. Here is that shockingly foreshadowing prophecy:

Psalm 22

My God, my God, why hast thou forsaken me? Why art thou so far from helping me, from the words of my groaning?

O my God, I cry by day, but thou dost not answer; and by night, but find no rest.

Yet thou art holy, enthroned on the praises of Israel.

In thee our fathers trusted; they trusted, and thou didst deliver them.

To thee they cried, and were saved; in thee they trusted, and were not disappointed.

But I am a worm, and no man; scorned by men, and despised by the people.

All who see me mock at me, they make mouths at me, they wag their heads;

"He committed his cause to the Lord; let him deliver him, let him rescue him, for he delights in him!"

Yet thou art he who took me from the womb; thou didst keep me safe upon my mother's breasts.

Upon thee was I cast from my birth, and since my mother bore me thou hast been my God.

Be not far from me, for trouble is near and there is none to help.

Many bulls encompass me, strong bulls of Bashan* surround me;

they open wide their mouths at me, like a ravening and roaring lion.

I am poured out like water, and all my bones are out of joint; my heart is like wax, it is melted within my breast;

my strength is dried up like a potsherd, and my tongue cleaves to my jaws; thou dost lay me in the dust of death.

Yea, dogs are round about me; a company of evildoers encircle me; they have pierced my hands and feet–

I can count all my bones——they stare and gloat over me;

they divide my garments among them, and for my raiment they cast lots.

But thou, O Lord, be not far off! O thou my help, hasten to my aid!

Deliver my soul from the sword, my life from the power of the dog!

Save me from the mouth of the lion, my afflicted soul from the horns of the wild oxen!

I will tell of thy name to my brethren; in the midst of the congregation I will praise thee:

You who fear the Lord, praise him! all you sons of Jacob, glorify him, and stand in awe of him, all you sons of Israel!

For he has not despised or abhorred the affliction of the afflicted; and he has not hid his face from him, but has heard, when he cried to him.

From thee comes my praise in the great congregation; my vows I will pay before those who fear him.

The afflicted shall eat and be satisfied; those who seek him shall praise the Lord! May your hearts live for ever!

All the ends of the earth shall remember and turn to the Lord; and all the families of the nations shall worship before him.

For dominion belongs to the Lord, and he rules over the nations.

Yea, to him shall all the proud of the earth bow down; before him shall bow all who go down to the dust, and he who cannot keep himself alive.

Posterity shall serve him; men shall tell of the Lord to the coming generation, and proclaim his deliverance to a people yet unborn, that he has wrought it.

[**My note:** The line, "strong bulls of Bashan," is a reference to the initial forces that came against Israel when they entered the Promise Land. *See* Deuteronomy 3:1.]

Judy assisted in young Jesus studying aboard during his teens, a portion of the so-called "lost years of Jesus," which we covered in detail in chapter 5. Here is where her close connections with the Magi made this all possible, for Judy herself had studied Eastern spirituality. Actually, when Cayce was asked where Judy got *her* education, he indicated that her mother and father contributed much to her understanding, along with her studies of Eastern wisdom, which broadened her mind and gave her a worldview, but her *primary* teacher was the Holy Spirit! (2067-11)

Through prayer, meditation, and quiet reflection, she received training from the Holy Spirit within her, as Jesus himself declared in John's Gospel: "The Counselor, the Holy Spirit, whom the Father will send in my name, he will teach you all things, and bring to your remembrance all that I have said to you." (John 14:26) Judy was using this same source in her process of enlightenment. Peter also supported this process when he wrote: "No prophecy ever came by the impulse of man, but men moved by the Holy Spirit spoken from God." (II Peter 1:21) Paul actually comes out and asks us, ""Do you not know that your body is a temple of the Holy Spirit within you, which you have from God?" (I Corinthians 6:19) Judy received her wisdom directly from the Holy Spirit. And Cayce explained that her colleagues were aware of her enlightened source, and this added to her being "accepted" as the leader of the Essenes at the Carmel temple.

In the present incarnation with Edgar Cayce, this is how Judy, now known and published under her name Judy Chandler, recorded her meeting with the famous psychic, known as *The Sleeping Prophet*:

During one of his [Edgar Cayce] periodic visits to New York I had made an appointment for what he termed a "Life Reading." When I walked into the room the famous clairvoyant stared at me in complete silence. I might have thought him exceedingly rude had I not been arrested by the astonishment which was spread over his face. It turned his eyes into two big question marks.

"Something the matter with me?" I demanded, when my nerves began a protest against his curious, silent regard.

"Yes," drawled the low voice of the distinguished Kentuckian, "there *is* something very *much* the matter with you—something I have never seen before in all my life."

"Please tell me," I urged impatiently.

"As you stand there I see a strong shaft of light flowing down from above you into your right side," he told me.

"My aura," I at once concluded, knowing that the ability to see auras was one of Edgar Cayce's numerous gifts.

"No," he corrected me promptly. 'This is not what is ordinarily called the aura. I see that too. It surrounds your head like a sunburst—rays of gold interspersed with lovely shades of blue. The shaft of light at your side is something else, something quite different. It is a blue-white radiance. I think it indicates spiritual sustenance and power. Maybe your Life Reading will explain it,' he suggested hopefully as he stretched himself out on his couch for the work at hand. His wife, Gertrude Cayce, sat beside him. Gladys Davis, his secretary, was ready with pad and pencil to record every word he uttered during his self-imposed hypnotic trance. In a few minutes it was evident that he was sound asleep, which was Mrs. Cayce's cue to submit the needed instructions to his Over-Self, or Soul-Mind as the readings themselves frequently described his superconscious state.

After giving my name in the here and now; my place and date of birth [May 5, 1880, Bowling Green, Virginia], Mrs. Cayce said:

"You will give the relation of this entity and the universe, and the universal forces; given the conditions which are as personalities, latent and exhibited, in the present life. You will also give the former appearances in the earth plane, giving time, place, and the name, and that in each life which built or retarded the entity. You will give the abilities of the present entity and that to which she may attain, and how. You will answer the questions she has submitted as I ask them."

That was a large order. But it was not too large for Edgar Cayce. Slowly he repeated my present name, the date and place of my birth, adding—after a slight pause—"Yes, we have the records here of that entity known as, or called, Julia Chandler—Judy."

Following this assurance that he had contacted the Akashic records of my former appearances on earth, as well as those on other planes between material incarnations, he proceeded to give me a detailed account of such experiences as it might be helpful to my present life and activities to know. [We'll read this reading shortly, but her recollection continues.]

When the reading ended, and Mr. Cayce resumed his normal state of consciousness, the first thing he wanted to know was whether or not anything was said which might explain the shaft of light pouring into my side.

"Don't you know?" I asked in astonishment, having assumed he would remember all information given.

"I rarely bring back any memory of anything that occurs during a reading," he explained. "Only a few times in the thousands I have given have I done so. I hope you got an explanation of the shaft of light?"

"No direct explanation," I had to admit. "Perhaps it lies in one of the incarnations you have just reported. I refer to the account of my sojourn in Palestine during the childhood and ministry of Jesus. If we may believe the information you have just given me, I was very close to Him then. Would you be willing to give me a full-time reading on just that particular period?" I asked.

Edgar Cayce gave me a characteristic smile. It began with his eyes and ended with his lips. It was an all-embracing, tender acquiescence to my request, and when—after two weeks—the further reading was given, it not only revealed the source of that shaft of light penetrating my side but also furnished the second occurrence which cemented one of the most valued and valuable friendships with which my present life has been blessed.

When Mrs. Cayce had given the suggestion which brought him out of his entranced state, Edgar rose slowly from the couch on which he had been lying, came over to me, stooped down, lifted my skirt and kissed its hem.

"What on earth are you doing that for?" I questioningly protested.

"To honor you for the rare and beautiful experience you have given me," he said. "I do not know what was in your reading but it must have been closely associated with Jesus the Christ for when I was through with the record of your Palestine experience at the time He was there, and turned back, *He* appeared to me—a glorious, radiant form. He placed his arm around my shoulder and said: 'Brother, I will walk with you a bit.' Thus He came with me all the way back to the gates of consciousness, and the path we trod was not just the tiny thread of light which usually guided me back, but a broad, brilliantly lighted pathway leading through realms of indescribable beauty, where heavenly strains of music filled the air. Do you wonder that I kiss the hem of your garment in honor and in gratitude for the most precious experience of a lifetime?"

My voice was choked with emotion as I reminded him that his experience had been the gift of the Master and had not come from me.

"Ah yes," he said, "the gift of my Lord, but only such a reading as you must have had could have lifted me to a vibration high enough to receive it."

Later, when he had read the typed report of what he had that day said in trance, he wrote me a letter from Virginia Beach in which he said:

"I am coming up to New York to give the hem of your dress another kiss for my walk with the Master at the close of your Palestine reading will always be a great influence in my life—and I do not mean just *this* life! Your intuitive guidance that this reading explains the shaft of light was certainly reliable since it makes it very clear to me that it emanates from the Christ, in which case I am sure it will strengthen, guide, and sustain you through all your present work, and uphold you in any crisis you may ever have to face."

Despite Judy's side-penetrating ray of light and her wonderful past-life experience with young Jesus, her life in this present incarnation with Edgar Cayce was not without suffering and disappointment. She was widowed twice due to illness in both her husbands and lost her thirteen-year-old son to illness as well. In her latter years she developed cancer and suffered pain until her death. And those who knew her found her to be a grouchy woman with a large ego, often critical and without much patience. During this lifetime she had been a famous radio host broadcasting from the then largest building in the world, the Empire State Building. She was the "Sky Lady" coming to you from the tallest building in the world. And this was in the glory days of radio, 1936 to 1945. Judy was the first woman to climb to the top of the Empire State Building! She was also a newspaper columnist, featured writer, drama critic, theatrical publicist, and lecturer. She eventually became a Trustee on the Board of Cayce's organization, the Association for Research and Enlightenment, and was the Regional Representative of the organization in New York for many years. It should be noted that when she was only six years old, she recalled a past life in ancient Greece as a disciple of Pythagoras (571–495 BCE)! Thus, she was already quite open to mystical teachings and reincarnation when she first met Edgar. Upon her death her body was buried in Washington DC on Palm Sunday, March 21, 1966.

Let's now read some of Cayce's readings for this important leader of the Essenes and teacher to young Jesus.

The following are Cayce's readings in the files at his center in Virginia Beach, Virginia, just as his longtime stenographer, Gladys Davis, took them down in shorthand and subsequently typed them with the exception that all-cap words are typed in italics. Again we have to keep in mind that the man Edgar Cayce did not speak in this King James biblical language, in fact he had a strong southern accent, but when giving his famous readings, it was "King James" English that came through him. And it is best if you follow his readings slowly, pausing to grasp what he said. Where I can, I'll help with "My note" asides.

This was Judy's first reading:

TEXT OF READING 1472-1
F 57 (Writer, Radio Broadcaster, Protestant)

This Psychic Reading given by Edgar Cayce at the David E. Kahn home, 20 Woods Lane, Scarsdale, N.Y., this 6th day of November, 1937, in accordance with request made by the self—Mrs. [1472], new Associate

Member of the Ass'n for Research & Enlightenment, Inc., recommended by Mr. [1151] and Mrs. [1158].

PRESENT
Edgar Cayce; Gertrude Cayce, Conductor; Gladys Davis, Steno. Mrs. [1472].

READING
Born May 5, 1880, in Bowling Green, Virginia.
Time of Reading 3:50 to 4:50 P. M. Eastern Standard Time. New York City.
(Life Reading Suggestion)
(In going back over years from present—"—'85—rather as a cross—'84, '83—" etc., on back to birth date.)

EC: Yes, we have the records here of that entity now known as or called [1472].

In giving the interpretations of these, we find these are those that may be helpful in the experience of the entity through the present sojourn.

These are beautiful in many of the experiences, yet the more turmoil may appear to be present in this present sojourn. [**My note:** And we have just gone over how much turmoil she experienced in this present lifetime with two husbands and her only son dying, and her life ending with the pain of cancer.]

For the entity has come a long way, and oft grows weary with the burdens not only that become a part of self's experience but that apparently are unburdened and yet burdened upon the entity, in its dealings with those about self.

Remember, though, that these *are* but that which is a part of the experience; for those whom He loveth, those He holdeth dear in their dealings with the fellow man.

For He hath indeed given His angels charge concerning thee, and He will bear thee up—if ye will faint not but hold to that purpose whereunto thou hast purposed in thy tabernacle in the present.

For know that His temple in thee is *holy*; and thy body-mind is indeed the temple of the living God.

Thus may ye find oft that upon the horns of the altar many of the burdens may be laid aside, and that the sweet incense of faith and hope and prudence and *patience* will arise to bring the consciousness and the awakening of the glories that may be thine.

In giving, for this entity, the interpretations of the records made—upon time and space from God's book of remembrance—we find life, as a whole, is a continuous thing; emanating from power, energy, God-Consciousness, ever.

And as it must ever be, so has it ever been; so that only a small vista or vision may be taken here and there, from the experiences of the entity in those environs of an astrological nature (as ye term).

Or the experiences of the visitation of the soul-entity, as it were, during those periods when absent from the material, three-dimensional matter, become as in the accord with that which has been accredited by the students—yea, by the seers of old to those astrological aspects.

[**My note:** As note earlier, Cayce's readings taught that souls are active between physical incarnations in realms associated with the planets in the solar system. Not in the three–dimensional reality but in fourth and fifth dimensional states of existence.]

That is, the influences or environs to the entity in those consciousnesses that are given as a portion of the experience, from such sojourns, are as signs or symbols or emblems in the experience of the entity in the present.

For as the entity experiences, it is ever the *now* and what the entity or soul may do *about* the consciousness or awareness that makes for those influences which are to be.

Hence such influences that are accredited much to the astrological aspects become a portion of the entity, not because of the position at the time of birth but because of the entity's sojourn there. Or, rather, because the All-Wise, All-Creative Force has given into the keeping of the souls that they journey as it were from experience or awareness or consciousness to consciousness, that they—as a portion of the whole—may become aware of same.

And as the injunction has been from the beginning, subdue ye the influences from without, that ye may be a fit companion, that you may be one with that Creative Force or Energy ye worship as thy Maker, thy God, thy Brother—yea, that within which ye live, ye move, ye have your being!

Then as we find, as the consciousness is aware of the individual now, and knows itself to be itself—these are the purposes.

Then only as an individual gives itself in service does it become aware. For as the divine love has manifested, does become manifested, that alone ye have given away do ye possess. That *alone* is the manner in which the growth, the awareness, the consciousness grows to be.

For until the experiences are thine, thy awareness cannot be complete.

As to the astrological aspects, we find these become as innate or mental—or dream, or visions, or cries, or voices as it were from within.

But the influences that arise from the few appearances in the material sojourns or consciousness (that have an effect in the present) are to create or bring about or affect the emotions.

[**My note:** Cayce has just stated that mental imagery and urges are often from one's planetary sojourns while emotions are from past incarnations in a physical body, with its hormones and nervous systems. Emotions are most often from past lives while mental urges and imagery are often from planetary sojourns between incarnations.]

Hence as there are those contacts with individual entities—for this entity is struggling even as they—there comes with the awareness of their thought-expression in material consciousness the emotions, the awareness of their struggles having been as parallel, or at cross purposes here or there.

Yet having left as it were upon the skein of time and space that consciousness that only in the patience of the divine love may that hope, that helpfulness be made complete—as ye lean upon the arm of thy Brother, thy Friend, ye may be borne to the very presence of divinity itself. [**My note:** Cayce's readings were big on loving one another, helping one another.]

In the astrological aspects then we find these as a part of this entity's experience; that Jupiter, Mars, Venus, Uranus, Neptune all become a portion of the entity's innate activity.

Hence these come into material manifestation by the application of, or doing something about, the urge produced by that activity that is latent yet is so subtle, yet so definite as to produce that which brings movement to the experience of self.

Thus it becomes a portion of its activity in the material sojourn.

Venus and Jupiter bring sympathy, love, beauty; and those abilities to depict same into material activity such that it becomes a portion of the longings and the hopes of the many.

For as thoughts are things, and as their currents run into the experience of individuals, they shape lives and activities so that they become miracles or crimes in the experiences of others as they mete them in their associations with their fellow men.

For as ye do it unto the least of these, thy brethren, ye do it unto thy Maker.

Hence these make for those activities in the experience of this entity's soul in which the masses, as well as classes and groups, are to be, will be, influenced.

Hence is there little wonder that oft there is the second thought—yea, the counsel with the inner self—as to whether that written, that spoken, that printed, that said in thy dealings with others becomes as a wonderment or is constructive or destructive?

But more and more may the thoughts expressed and given out by the entity bring constructive activity in the lives of others, as the self gains that open consciousness that He has given His angels charge lest ye dash thy foot against a stone. [**My note:** This is referring to the statement in Psalm 91:11 and repeated in Matthew 4:6.]

Hence know that He is in His holy temple, and that all the earth must hear, must know. For every knee must bow to that love divine, as ye are capable of meting and measuring through such activities in thy experience and thy relationships with thy fellow men.

In Mars we find those fits of anger, resentment, selfishness here and there; those impure motives creating those struggles, those entanglements, those angers. Yet these as they arise upon thy horizon of activity in thy relationships may oft keep from view the visions of that glory prepared for those who love the Lord.

Yet know that truth and light, as may be aroused or made alive from the assurances of His walks with thee, will dissipate those fogs, those mists, as ye apply love in thy dealings with every character of circumstance in thy experience with others.

Then these will matter little; for the Lord's ways are not past finding out, yet ye must oft learn to wait upon the Lord, and not become overanxious—in thy anxiety that "they, too" taste of the goodness that may be found in the divine love.

In Uranus, as well as in Neptune, we find the water—yea, the elementals;

the fire and water—oft interfering? no, cleansing rather. For as hath been given, all must be tried so as by fire. All must be purified. [**My note:** It is a widespread classic teaching and initiation that one is first cleansed through absolution using water (as in baptism) and then in fiery purification by the Spirit. As John the Baptist explained: "I indeed baptize you in water unto repentance: but he that comes after me is mightier than I, whose shoes I am not worthy to bear; he shall baptize you in the Holy Spirit and in fire." (Matthew 3:11) And Paul wrote: "Our God is a consuming fire!" (Hebrews 12:29)]

Yet in the beauty of life springing anew in the water of life itself, ye find in the mysteries—yea, the occult and the spiritual forces—influences that make for *extremes* in the lives of many. [**My note:** Extremes is a classical characteristic of the Uranian influence.]

Yet as He walked the path to Gethsemane, [Jesus] as He struggled alone with His own Cross; so ye—as ye struggle *have* the assurance that His presence abideth; and they that become overzealous or overanxious may find that the stepping-stones that may be in thy experience become stumbling-stones.

But keep ye the faith in not the Cross as sacrifice but the Cross as the *way*, the *light*, the *life!*

For without the Cross there is not the Crown! [**My note:** In another reading Cayce developed this idea further: "Crucify desire in self; that ye may be awakened to the real abilities of helpfulness that lie within thy grasp." (2475-1)]

As to the appearances in the earth, all may not be visioned from this particular experience or sojourn. For as ye apply thyself in thy daily experiences in bringing those bonds here, those activities in the sojourns of others, ye bring the *new* visions and vistas of thy sojourns materially as well as in the astrological spheres about this thine own concept of the universe. But:

Before this we find the entity was in the land of the present nativity [born in Virginia], during those periods of the settlings in the early portions of the land.

It was when there were those being brought into the land for companions, helpmeets to those of the land.

The entity was among those brought hither from the English land, and become in the household of that family which later grew to be in authority, in power, in that Virginian land; or in the household of that family whose name has been changed to what is now called Byrd—then Bayonne [?]. [**My note:**

With their families, Christopher Byrd arrived in Virginia in 1651, William Byrd in 1653, and John Byrd in 1677.]

In the experience, as Clementine, the entity's activities were in the assurance of the freedom of actions for the bringing not only of conveniences into the home but into the activities of the neighboring groups roundabout.

And these have left upon the consciousness of the entity such emotions that oft it finds itself bound by convention, bound by that which prevents the full expression.

Yet know in the awareness that ye will find more and more that the *truth* indeed sets one *free*. *Not* to convention, of the material policies or activities, but in *spirit and in truth*!

For God looks upon the purposes, the ideals of the heart, and not upon that which men call convention.

Before that we find the entity was in the Palestine land, during those days when the Master walked in the earth; and when there were the peoples about those activities of not only the birth but His sojourns before and after the return from Egypt—those whom Judy blessed, that labored in the preserving of the records of *his* activities as the Child; the activities of the Wise Men, the Essenes and the groups to which Judy had been the prophetess, the healer, the writer, the recorder—for all of these groups.

And though questioned or scoffed by the Roman rulers and the tax gatherers, and especially those that made for the levying or the providing for those activities for the taxation, the entity gained throughout.

Though the heart and body was often weary from the toils of the day, and the very imprudence—yea, the very selfishness of others for the aggrandizing of their bodies rather than their souls or minds seeking development, the entity grew in grace, in knowledge, in understanding.

And in the present those abilities arise from its desire, from its hopes to put into the word of the *day*, the experience of the day, in all phases of human experience, *lessons*—yea, symbols, yea tenets—that will drive as it were *home*, in those periods when the soul takes thought and counsel with itself, as to whence the experiences of the day are leading—as to whether they are leading to those activities that are the fruits of the spirit of truth and life, or to those that make for selfishness, and the aggrandizement of material appetites without thought of those things that are creative and only make the pure growths within the experience of others.

Hence whether it be in jest, in stories, in song or poem, or whether in skits that may show the home life, the lover—yea, the weary traveler yea the high-minded, and they that think better of themselves than they ought to think—*these* abilities are there. Use them. For He, even as then, will bless thee with His presence in same. And what greater assurance can there be in the experience of any soul than to know that He—yea, the Son of Mary— yea, the Son of the Father, the Maker of heaven and earth, the Giver of all good gifts—will be thy right hand, yea thy heart, thy mind, thy eye, thy heart itself—if ye will hold fast to Him!

Before that we find the entity was in the Egyptian land, during those periods when there were the gatherings of those from the turmoils, from the banishments, and those from the Atlantean land. [**My note:** Here Cayce is referring to time when a remnant group of sinking Atlantis arrived in Egypt seeking refuge and when a high priest and his entourage were temporarily banished from Egypt by the pharaoh for violating standing rules. They were later happily received back into temple service by the same pharaoh. Apparently, Judy's soul was involved in both of these events. Cayce dates these events surprisingly early, around 10,000 BCE! Now with the dating of Gobekli Tepe to around 12,000 BCE, this Egyptian date may be possibly correct.]

The entity then was among those from the lands that were later called the Parthenian lands [ancient Greece], or what ye know as the Persian land from which the conquerors then of Egypt had come. [**My note:** That conquer of Egypt, who came from Persia, was Alexander the Great (21 July 356 BCE – 10 or 11 June 323 BCE). He conquered Persia in 334 BCE and two years later conquered Egypt in 332 BCE. Apparently, Judy's soul was among Alexander's people.]

As a Princess from that land the entity came to study the mysteries for the service it might give to those of her own land, the Carpathians or as has been given, the entity was among the *first* of the pure white from that land to seek from the Priest [Egyptian] and those activities in the Temple Beautiful for the purifying of self that she, too, might give to her own not only the tenets but the practical application of that which would bring home in the material experience an *assurance* in the separations from the body.

[**My note:** Cayce explained that the "Carpathians" of the Carpathian Mountains were also those from the Caucasus Mountains, thus "caucasians" or white-race people. Both mountain ranges were the origin of the white race. The original location of the black race according to

Cayce was Nubia (where all the gold in Egypt came—now the region of Lake Nasser in Aswan and portions of northern Sudan), the red race was Atlantis, the yellow race was the Gobi (but it was not a desert then but a lush high mountain plain, and Cayce predicted that we will find a "golden temple" beneath the sands of the Gobi), and the brown race was the Andes Mountain range in South America, the longest continental mountain range in the world, in seven nations: Ecuador, Chile, Colombia, Perú, Argentina, Bolivia, and Venezuela!]

Thus in the abilities of the entity from that experience, as well as those gained throughout those activities, we find in the present: Just meting out day by day those visions, that ye have gained here, that ye have seen in thy experiences, thy sojourns, ye will find that *he* the keeper, *he* the Creator, will give the increase necessary for the activities in every sphere of thy experience.

For keeping inviolate that thou knowest gives assurance not only in self but in the promises that He will bear thee *up*!

If there is kept that purpose in self, there is little need for a return; save as one that may lead the way to those that are still in darkness.

As to the practical application, then:

In the writing, in the song; in the meting it out in the conversation day by day. For *ye* can only be the sower. *God* giveth the increase!

Faint not at well-doing.

Ready for questions.

(Q) How can I extend the borders of my consciousness to include fourth dimensional knowledge and achieve greater spiritual illumination?

(A) These illuminations, the greater visions, only come by the communion with the true life and light from within.

For as thy body is the temple of thy *own* self, so is the kingdom of heaven within, even as He gave. And if ye will but open the door of thy consciousness and let Him come in, He will sup with thee and give thee that thou may *use* day by day.

(Q) Where, when and what was my relationship to the entity now known as [1470], in any past incarnation, and what does he mean to my present life pattern?

(A) In the Palestine period the self was as Judy, the entity [1470, a fellow broadcaster at the Empire State Building] was as the Roman that made light much, and later came to seek.

And thus in authority in self doth he find that those activities in the present will become much in the same way and manner. For not as one dependent upon the other, but one as bolstering as it were the purposes that may be held aright.

(Q) Where, when and what was my past relationship to the entity now known as [1151], and what is the purpose of my present association with him?

(A) In the same land.

Here we find quite a variation in the activity. For as the entity that walked in the way to Emmaus *found* that those records of those activities became part and parcel of the experience, so is that bond of sympathy found in the associations that awakens the urge for a *helpfulness without question* as one to another. [**My note:** Cayce's readings for 1151, one of the two who walked with Jesus on the road to Emmaus, explain that 1151 had been in Rome on business during the crucifixion and did not return until days after the resurrection. Because 1151 had such a heartfelt love for Jesus, he and his partner actually "drew" the resurrection Jesus to them. Here's some of this: "Then as they sat at meat, as He brake the bread (that represents His broken body), there came the knowledge that they spoke with the Master. Hence an experience which may draw this very near to the entity in the present: How oft in thine experience has there come to thy inmost knowledge the *real, real* purpose of individuals as ye broke bread with them! Not that this then becomes as an omen. It is a *reality*; for ye broke bread with *life* itself! And as it represents the staff of life, as it represents His body, how *much*, how oft, how great is the influence in thine experience of those ye break bread with!" (1151-4)]

(Q) Is radio the field in which I can best use my spiritual enlightenment and writing ability for the greatest service to the world?

(A) Radio is a means of expression; writing is a means of confirmation and is longer *lasting*.

(Q) Why do I get so little love, consideration and appreciation from those to whom I pour out the most service and devotion?

(A) Study that which has been given thee relative to such, and ye will see that it is patience ye must learn, that ye must add to those virtues that have made thee ever the burden bearer for the many throughout those periods when the awakenings were coming.

Faint not because of thy loneliness, for who can be alone with His love, His promises abiding with thee!

These may make for a blooming into activity in thy experience, and *will*, if ye will give expression more and more to those promises that are thy very own.

For He, as He hath promised, may bring to thy remembrance *all* things—from the foundations of the earth. Know the Lord is nigh; and that those who keep watch, who keep faith *with* thee, are even as those of old—when there are the hundreds, yea the thousands that have never bended the knee to Baal, but as thee—only need that light, that assurance that He *is* the guiding light!

(Q) How can I help my daughter, the entity now known as [. . .]?

(A) Be not overanxious. Ever be ready rather to give an answer for the faith that lieth within. Not as argumentative, but as that which has been, which is, which ever will be the assurance to thee of the faith, the love that conquers all.

(Q) Who and where is my real mate?

(A) This may best be found by considering that as was the experience in those activities during the Palestine period, yea those full activities of the entity *as* Judy in that period with the Essenes. Study even that little which has been preserved of same. Ye will find him studying same also!

(Q) Can you tell me anything of the activity and development of my son, the entity known in this life as [. . .] who died at the age of 13?

(A) As has been given thee, let Him, the Way, the Life, reveal this to thee in thine *own* meditation. He is near at hand.

If thine eyes will be opened, if thy purposes will be set in the service, in the patience of love, He may reveal—as given—*all* things to thee.

Let thy deeper meditation be, in thine own way, but as these thoughts:

"Lord, my Lord, my God! Thy handmaid seeks light and understanding! Open to my mind, my heart, my purpose, that which I may use in my daily service, my daily contacts, that will be more and more expressive of thy love to the children of men."

We are through for the present.

Copy to Self, Ass'n file

Two weeks later Judy got a second reading from Cayce. Here it is:

TEXT OF READING 1472-3
F 57 (Writer, Radio Broadcaster, Protestant)

This Psychic Reading given by Edgar Cayce at the David E. Kahn home, 20 Woods Lane, Scarsdale, N.Y., this 18th day of November, 1937, in accordance with request made by the self—Mrs. [1472] new Active Member of the Ass'n for Research & Enlightenment, Inc.

PRESENT

Edgar Cayce; Gertrude Cayce, Conductor; Gladys Davis, Steno. Mrs. [1472].

READING

Time of Reading 3:55 to 4:50 P. M. Eastern Standard Time. New York City.

GC: You will have before you the entity, Mrs. [1472], born . . . , who seeks detailed information concerning her Palestine sojourn as Judy, covering her biographical life, work and associations throughout that experience, from the entity's entrance to her departure. You will also give the developing or retarding associations and influences of that plane which bear on the present life, and how they may be best used in the present experience for the entity's highest development and service. You will then answer the questions she will submit, as I ask them, concerning her present life and associations.

EC: Yes, we have the records here of that entity now called Mrs. [1472]!

Here we may give even portions of the records as scribed by the entity called Judy, as the teacher, as the healer, as the prophetess through that experience.

Some four and twenty years before the advent of that entity, that soul-entrance into material plane called Jesus, we find Phinehas (?) and Elkatma (?) making those activities among those of the depleted group of the prophets in Mount Carmel; that begun by Samuel, Elisha, Elijah, Saul, and those during those early experiences.

Because of the divisions that had arisen among the peoples into sects, as the Pharisee, the Sadducee and their divisions, there had arisen the Essenes that had cherished not merely the conditions that had come as word of mouth but had kept the records of the periods when individuals had been visited with the supernatural or out of the ordinary experiences; whether in dreams, visions, voices, or what not that had been and were felt by these students of the customs, of the law, of the activities throughout the experiences of this peculiar people—the promises and the many ways these had been interpreted by those to whom the preservation of same had been committed.

Hence we find Phinehas and the companion, both having received the experience similar to that received by Hannah and Elkanah, had drawn aside from many of the other groups.

And then as in answer to that promise, the child—Judy—was born.

That the entity was a daughter, rather than being a male, brought some disturbance, some confusion in the minds of many.

Yet the life, the experiences of the parents had been such that still—fulfilling their promise—they brought the life of their child, Judy, and dedicated it to the study and the application of self to the study of those things that had been handed down as a part of the *experiences* of those who had received visitations from the unseen, the unknown—or that worshiped as the Divine Spirit moving into the activities of man.

Hence we find the entity Judy was brought up in that environment; not of disputations, not of argumentations, but rather as that of rote and writ—as was considered necessary for the development, the influences, the activities of the life, to induce or to bring about those experiences.

That much had been to that period as tradition rather than as record, appeared—from the activity of the entity, Judy—to have made a great impression.

So there was the setting about to seek means and manners for the preservation, and for the making of records of that which had been handed down as word of mouth, as tradition. Such channels and ways were sought out. And eventually the manner was chosen in which records were being kept in Egypt rather than in Persia, from which much of the tradition arose—of course—because of the very indwelling of the peoples in that land.

Hence not only the manners of the recording but also the traditions of Egypt, the traditions from India, the conditions and traditions from many of the Persian lands and from many of the borders about same, became a part of the studies and the seeking of the entity Judy early in the attempts to make, keep and preserve such records.

The manners of communication being adverse, owing to the political situations that gradually arose due to the Roman influence in the land, made more and more a recluse of the entity in its early periods; until there were those visitations by what ye call the Wise Men of the East—one from Persia, one from India, one from the Egyptian land.

These reasoned with the Brethren, but more was sought from the studies of the entity Judy at that experience.

Then there was the report by the Wise Men to the king. Has it been thought of, or have you heard it reasoned as to why the Wise Men went to Herod, who was only second or third in authority rather than to the Romans who were *all* authority in the land?

Because of Judy; knowing that this would arouse in the heart and mind of this debased ruler—that only sought for the aggrandizement of self—such reactions as to bring to him, this despot, turmoils with those then in authority.

Why? There was not the proclamation by the Wise Men, neither by Judy nor the Essenes, that this new king was to replace Rome! It was to replace the Jewish authority in the land!

Thus we find, as it would be termed in the present, attention was called or pointed to the activity of the Essenes such that a little later—during those periods of the sojourn of the Child in Egypt because of same—Herod issued the edict for the destruction.

This brought to those that were close to the entity those periods that were best described by the entity itself, in the cry of Rachel for her children that were being born into a period of opportunity—yet the destructive forces, by the very edict of this tyrant, made them as naught.

Hence during those periods of the ministry of John, and then of Jesus, more and more questioning was brought upon the recorder—or Judy—by the Roman authorities, or the Roman spies, or those who were the directors of those who collected and who registered taxes of those peoples for the Roman collection.

Consequently, we find the entity came in contact with the Medes, the Persians, the Indian influence of authority—because of the commercial association as well as the influence that had been upon the world by those activities of Saneid and those that were known during the periods of Brahma and Buddha.

These brought to the experience of the entity the weighing of the counsels from the traditions of the Egyptians and of her own kind—and then that new understanding.

Hence we find the entity in those periods soon after the Crucifixion not only giving comfort but a better interpretation to the Twelve, to the Holy Women; an understanding as to how Woman was redeemed from a place of obscurity to her place in the activities of the affairs of the race, of the world, of the empire—yea, of the home itself.

Those all became a part of the entity's experiences during that portion.

Hence we find many have been, many are, the contacts the entity has made and must make in this present experience.

For, as then, the evolution of man's experiences is for the individual purpose of becoming more and more acquainted with those activities in the relationships with the fellow man, as an exemplification, as a manifestation of Divine Love—as was shown by the Son of man, Jesus; that *each* and every soul *must become, must be,* the *savior* of some soul! to even *comprehend* the purpose of the entrance of the Son *into* the earth—that man might have the closer walk with, yea the open door to, the very heart of the living God!

The entity's activities during the persecutions aroused much in the minds of those that made war again and again upon the followers of the Nazarene, of Jesus, of the Apostles here and there.

And the entity, as would be termed, was hounded, yea was persecuted the more and more; yet remaining until what ye would call the sixty-seventh year *after* the Crucifixion; or until Time itself began to be counted from same.

For the records as were borne by the entity, it will be found, were *begun* by the activities of the entity during what ye would term a period sixty years *after* the Crucifixion.

And then they were reckoned first by the peoples of Carmel, and then by the brethren in Antioch, then a portion of Jerusalem, then to Smyrna, Philadelphia, and those places where these were becoming more active.

The entity—though receiving rebuffs, yea even stripes in the body—died a natural death in that experience; at the age then of ninety-one.

As to the associations, the lessons that are to be gained in the applications of self from that experience:

Many are the urges that arise, as indicated; many are the impulses oft to feel that the very knowledge puts self in a position to condemn.

But condemn not, even as He did not condemn.

Again there are the inclinations that arise for abilities to present, to correlate, subjects that are truths hidden in tradition, hidden in prejudice of race, hidden in tradition of the patriotic influences that are accredited by the very spirit of a nation of people, or a custom, or a condition that has set itself in order as organizations.

But gathering these, do not condemn. For know, there is only *one spir-*

it—that is the Spirit of Truth that has growth within same! For if there is the spirit of strife, or the spirit of any activities that bring about contention or turmoils, it takes hold upon those very fires that ye have so *well* put away; yet that keep giving giving—urges that are spoken of, even as He that ye *know*, that the prince of this world is as a raging lion, going about seeking whom he may destroy!

What is this spirit then of unrest but that very cry, as He gave in that triumphal entry, "If ye did not cry Hosanna, glory to the Lord, the king of kings, the very stones would cry out!"

That these overreach themselves, ye have seen in the great white light of thine understanding, of the many *varied* feelings, yea the very varied approaches ye have seen.

Does it become any wonder to thee, knowing, feeling that ye have known these experiences, that ye have heard many a voice raised here and there, crying "Lo, here am I—*lo*, here is the way—*lo*—Listen!"

But rather as those promises, yea as thy very self hath *pronounced*, "It is the still small voice within that finds communion with that Spirit that beareth witness that thy interpretation be true," that all the prophets pronounced Him as that star spoken of, as that voice raised in the wilderness, as the star of Jacob, yea of the household of David, yea as of Judah that lion that will bring that as He declared unto the world—"My peace I leave with thee."

That ye declared, that hold to!

For there *is* no other way than that each soul be awakened to that ye did proclaim to the earth, "Behold He cometh with power and might and ye shall know Him as He *is*: for He convicts thee of thy purpose among thy fellow men!"

Ready for questions.

(Q) How close was my association with Jesus in my Palestine sojourn?

(A) A portion of the experience the entity was the teacher!

How close? So close that the very heart and purposes were proclaimed of those things that were traditions! For the entity sent Him to Persia, to Egypt, yea to India, that there might be completed the more perfect knowledge of the material ways in the activities of Him that became the Way, the Truth!

(Q) How can I extend the scope of my writing opportunity to use this ability in more important channels and wider service than at present?

(A) As may be gathered from that as given, by putting into first thine own experience, thine own activity, those teachings of Him; not as tenets but as *living* experiences! So manifesting same in the lives and minds of those whom the self may meet day by day, learning that lesson as He so well manifested, that it was not in the separation as John, not in the running away as Elijah, not as in sitting in high places as Isaiah, not as in that form of Jeremiah—mourning; not in that lording as Moses—but *all things unto all men!* reaching them in their own plane of experience; and not with long-facedness!

For as He—He wined, He dined with the rich, He consorted with the poor, He entered the temple on state occasions; yea He slept in the field with the shepherds, yea He walked by the seashore with the throngs, He preached to those in the mount—*all things*; and yet ever ready to present the tenets, the truths, even in those forms of tales, yea parables, yea activities that took hold upon the *lives of men and women* in *every* walk of human experience!

So ye will find that the lessons ye gave then may be used today! Why? Because Truth is *truth, ever*—in *whatever stage*, in whatever realm of evolution, in *whatever* realm ye find same; it is as He gave—the little leaven.

Think not, even as He, to do some great deed that would make the welkin ring throughout the earth. Rather *know* it is the little line, the little precept, the little lesson given into the lives and experiences that brings the awareness into the hearts and souls of men and women; that consciousness of the *nearness* in the still small voice within.

For as proclaimed of old, it is not in the thunder or lightning, it is not in the storm, it is not in the loudness—but the still small voice within!

So as ye write, so as ye talk, so as ye love—let it be in meekness of spirit, in *purposefulness* of service, in an activity and an eye single to the *glory* of the Father through those that are His children.

For "Who is my mother, my brother, my sister? They that do the will of the Father, the same is my mother, my brother, my sister."

What is the will? Love the Lord with all thy heart, thy mind, thy body; thy neighbor as thyself!

Sow the seeds of kindness, helpfulness, longsuffering, gentleness, patience, brotherly love; and leave the *increase* to the Father, who *alone* can give same either in the spirit, the mind *or* the body!

Being patient even as He.

This is the manner in which ye may reach, O the whole earth, even as ye did—Judy—in thy counsel as given thee by thy father then in the flesh, as ye learned, as ye gathered from the counsel of the lessons from the patriarchs of old, by the lessons of tradition that ye first—even as he—set to be in order; yea have heard as of old, an eye for an eye, a tooth for a tooth; ye have heard he that does the good, do the good to him; but "I say, he that would smite thee on the right cheek, *turn thou* the other also! He that would sue thee and take away thy cloak, give him thy coat also."

Did ye not set these as the very words given by Him who is the Lord of Lords and the King of Kings?

For to him who hath overcome—and He standeth at the door and knocks—and ye, as all His servants, His children, His sisters, His brethren—may be co-laborers with Him in the harvest that is ripe.

(Q) What is the purpose of my present business position and when will I be freed from it?

(A) That ye may reach the more. Each experience, as ye will learn the more and more—as ye see them, just as given—is that ye may serve the better. For how gave He? "He that is greatest among you is servant of all."

When shall ye be free from same? When ye have attained, when ye have gained that next step that He may say, "Move on, now; that thy children, those ye have taught, may carry on. Ye are called to the greater service of making known again—by word of mouth or by the pen—the greater lessons of Truth."

We are through for the present.

Copy to Self—Special Delivery, Ass'n file

Judy received sixteen readings from Edgar Cayce until his passing in 1945. But the two that we just read were the key ones for her Essene incarnation and our focus here. However, Mrs. 2067 received a reading in which the Essenes were commented on, among several other interesting events and ideas. Let's review that reading:

TEXT OF READING 2067-11
F 56 (Teacher, Quaker-Spiritualist)
This Psychic Reading given by Edgar Cayce at the office of the Association, Arctic Crescent, Virginia Beach, Va., this 22nd day of February, 1943, in accordance with request made by the self—Dr. [2067], Associate Member of the Ass'n for Research & Enlightenment, Inc.

PRESENT
Edgar Cayce; Hugh Lynn Cayce, Conductor; Gladys Davis, Steno.

READING

Time of Reading . . . College, 11:00 to 11:40 A. M. Eastern War Time . . . , Vermont.

HLC: You will have before you the Christ Ministry book being prepared by [2067], . . . College, . . . , Vermont. You will ans. the ques. the entity submits, as I ask them, regarding the history and material needed to complete this book:

EC: Yes, we have the information that has been indicated, and those efforts on the part of [2067] to put this into a story.

Ready for questions.

(Q) For the title of the Christ Ministry book will *Jesus, the Essene* be acceptable?

(A) It would be to some, but to more it would not.

(Q) Would you suggest a suitable title?

(A) Who's writing the book? From here, or from the compilations? It would be preferable that the data be prepared, and then *from* that there may be indicated the better title. The Early Ministry, or the Early Life, or the Life of Jesus as the Essene, not Jesus the Essene.

(Q) For literary purposes, please describe a secret Essene meeting before Christ, at which, or her parents, or Thesea, or some Bible characters were present.

(A) This might be described very well as by any authentic meeting of certain groups founded by Solomon. But the description should not be from here, for it would be quite at variance to much of the data prepared. Draw upon the own imagination.

The Essenes were a group of individuals sincere in their purpose, and yet not orthodox as to the rabbis of that particular period. Thus such a meeting would be described by the meditations, certain ritualistic formulas, as may be outlined very well from some of those activities as may be gathered from the activities of the priest in the early period when there was the establishing of the tabernacle.

Remember, recall, the first two didn't do so well, even under the direction of the high priest; for they offered strange fire.

Let not, then, that as would be offered here, become as strange fire, but as in keeping with the precept of Jesus, "I and the Father are one;" not individually, but in the personal application of the tenets, commandments, being one in purpose, one in application.

Thus such a meeting would be the interpreting of each promise that has been made; as to when, as to how there would come the Promised One.

Analyze in the mind, then, that from the 3rd of Genesis through to the last even of Malachi. Set them aside. Use them as the basis of discussions, as the various groups may be set in order; each rotating as a teacher, as an instructor for that particular meeting; remembering all were secret meetings.

(Q) Tell of the work, the prophecies, the hopes of Phinehas and Elkatma, Judy's parents, at Carmel, as Essenes.

(A) These were those activities that may be illustrated very well in the ministry of the parents of the strong man—that a parallel may be drawn; as to how first there was the appearance to the mother, and then the father, as to what should be the ministry, the activity of the entity that was to lead that group, and aid in the early teaching of the prophecies of the life of the child Jesus, as well as of John. For, John was more the Essene than Jesus. For Jesus held rather to the spirit of the law, and John to the letter of same.

(Q) Was Judy immaculately conceived, as perhaps was Samuel?

(A) Neither were immaculately conceived.

(Q) In Jewish history was anybody but Mary and Jesus immaculately conceived?

(A) Mary was not immaculately conceived [according to Jewish history]. Jesus was. There have been others, but not in Jewish history. [GD's note: EC made an appointment 3/27/43 to clarify contradictory statements in re Mary but had to cancel due to rush of emergency rdgs. Dr. [2067] had on 2/27/43 requested Ck. Life on her Salem incarnation, which rdg. was gotten in 8/43 under 2067-12. Too bad we did not get the rdg. clarifying the Mary statements instead. 4/19/43 EC wrote that he was swamped with appointments, HL had gone into the army, and he didn't know when he'd be able to get another rdg. on the Christ ministry material.]

(Q) Why was Judy not a boy as expected?

(A) That is from the powers on high, and gave the first demonstration of woman's place in the affairs and associations of man. For, as were the teachings of Jesus, that released woman from that bondage to which she had been held since the ideas of man conceived from the fall of Eve, or of her first acceptance of the opinions—these were the first, and those activities that brought about, in the teachings materially, that as Jesus proclaimed.

(Q) For what purposes was Judy sent into the world at that time?

(A) Just indicated.

(Q) Describe any outstanding points or unusual abilities Judy had.

(A) Only as one brought into those activities—as it may be well described as the feminine of Samson.

(Q) Where did Judy receive her education, in what subjects, and who were her teachers?

(A) The Holy Spirit, and the mother and father; not from other sources, though there were those activities from all of the teachings of the East, through those early periods before there were those acceptances of Judy as the leader of the Essenes at Carmel at that period.

(Q) During the lifetime of Jesus where did Judy live and with whom?

(A) In Carmel; with the companion and the mother.

(Q) Please describe Judy's personal appearance, her dress, her personality, her faith.

(A) Draw upon the imagination for these. As would be the dress of Samson, making it feminine.

(Q) Tell of Judy's marriage, the name of her husband, his work—names of children and their accomplishments.

(A) His work had to do with the records that were translated for the various groups. The activities of Judy through these experiences were much as might be termed those of Hannah, during those periods when there were those seekings for that from the Lord that might give a recompense for those doubts brought out by others.

(Q) What were the names of Judy's children?

(A) These have little to do with that needed. This has been indicated.

(Q) What were the "fears" that wrecked Judy's son who is now [2795] and why was Judy, the healer, unable to heal him?

(A) It was not disease, other than that within self. Why were Samuel's sons sinners? These may only be answered within the individual or from the seeking of the individual himself.

(Q) Tell about the angels appearing to Judy, when, where, and what they said.

(A) Which period? These were many and oft.

(Q) Please describe Judy's home life as well as her Essene activities.

(A) That as might be the description of an individual who had set self aside as a channel for such activities. These are very hard to be understood from the material mind, or from the material understanding or concept, especially in this period of consciousness. For, then man walked close with God. When there were those preparations—it is possible in the present, but not *acceptable*. Consequently, to describe the home life as to say they sat in the sun, ate three square meals a day and wore little or nothing, or that they dressed in the best—it must be that as from the spirit. May best be described as given by Luke, in his description of those things that disturbed Mary. "She kept these things and pondered them in her heart." She kept those experiences, those teachings—she pondered them in her heart. This did not prevent her from being, then, a material person, nor one with the faculties and desires for material associations—as indicated in the lack of celibacy. Is this indicated in any condition in the book, or man's relationship to God? Nowhere is this indicated!

(Q) Tell about Judy teaching Jesus, where and what subjects she taught him, and what subjects she planned to have him study abroad.

(A) The prophecies! Where? In her home. When? During those periods from his twelfth to his fifteenth-sixteenth year, when he went to Persia and then to India. In Persia, when his father died. In India when John first went to Egypt—where Jesus joined him and both became the initiates in the pyramid or temple there.

(Q) What subjects did Judy plan to have him study abroad?

(A) What you would today call astrology.

(Q) At what major events in Jesus' life was Judy present—such as casting out of demons, healing, feeding 5,000, etc.?

(A) At his teaching—for a period of some five years.

(Q) Was she present at any of the healings or the feeding of the multi-tudes?

(A) Those where she chose to, but she was very old then. She lived to be sufficiently old to know, of course, of the feeding of the first five thousand. She was present, but rather as one that brought the crowds together, than as contributing to the activities at the time. For, there the divisions arose, to be sure.

(Q) Was Judy present at the Crucifixion or the Resurrection?

(A) No. In spirit—that is, in mind—present. For, remember, Judy's experience at that time was such that she might be present in many places without the physical body being there!

(Q) Tell of instances when Judy and Thesea, the Essene, worked or planned together.

(A) Only at the regular periods, or meetings of the Essenes, as we find. We are covering too great a period here. Draw something on the self! We are through for the present.

Copy to Self, Mrs. [1472], Ass'n file

Chapter 8

Two Sons of the Essenes: John the Baptist and Jesus of Nazareth

The Forerunner, John the Baptist

Intimately connected with the story of Jesus is the story of John the Baptist, who, as we know, is the son of Elizabeth and Zechariah (some translations render his name as Zacharias, with varying spellings). Zechariah was a priest serving in the Great Temple in Jerusalem. Elizabeth was the cousin of Jesus' mother. John was born a few months before Jesus and therefore would have had to have been sent out of the land to avoid Herod's death order to kill all boy babies under the age of two years. It is likely that only he and his mother fled to Egypt, because his father, being an active priest in the Temple, would not have been able to be gone out of the country for such an extended time. Sadly, John's father was murdered by the Sanhedrin when they discovered his ties to the Essenes. John's mother dies when he is only twelve. In Matthew 3, we learn that John becomes an ascetic nomad whose diet (locusts and wild honey), dress (camel's hair and leather), and message ("Repent, for the Kingdom of Heaven is at hand!") attracted many who were seeking repentance and renewal. Matthew's Gospel identifies John as the one spoken of in Isaiah 40:3–5, "A voice cries: 'In the wilderness prepare the way of the Lord, make straight in the desert a highway for our God. Every valley shall be lifted up, and every mountain and hill be made low; the uneven ground shall become level, and the rough places a plain. And the glory of the Lord shall be revealed, and all flesh shall see it together, for the mouth of the Lord has spoken.'"

John was certainly a voice crying in the wilderness. His ministry was not among the people and their towns, synagogues, or the Temple, but in the Judean desert and the Jordan steppes. Yet, from these remote areas his voice and message carried far, drawing many to hear him and receive his baptism, and drawing the wrath of those in authority whom he often chastised. Historian Josephus characterizes him as a moralizer with a washing ritual (baptism), which reflects the opinion of the authorities of that time.

But the Gospel of John identifies him as the prophesied forerunner of the Messiah. This prophecy is found in Malachi 4:5, "Behold, I will send you Elijah the prophet before the great and terrible day when the Lord comes." John's manner and appearance reflects the spirit and style that were so naturally Elijah. Elijah first appears in 1 Kings 17. He is identified as a Tishbite, meaning that he was from Tishbi, a place in Upper Galilee, which is mentioned in the Jewish apocryphal book of Tobit. He journeyed from Tishbi into Gilead, a mountainous region east of Jordan. However, the historian Josephus supposes that Tishbi was some place in the land of Gilead (Ant. 8:13, 2). It has been identified by some with el-Ishtib, a place some twenty-two miles south of the Sea of Galilee, among the mountains of Gilead. Whatever the case, all of this area is wilderness, and Elijah is guided, as is John, by God to live in the wilderness and deliver His message to the rulers in the surrounding towns. God instructs Elijah to live by "the brook Cherith, that is before the Jordan. It shall be, that you shall drink of the brook; and I have commanded the ravens to feed you there." (1 Kings 1:1–6) The ravens bring Elijah bread in the morning and the evening. Elijah is directed to go to the Jewish king Ahab, who has wrongfully married a daughter not of Israel, none other than the famous Jezebel, and he has built altars to her god, Baal. The parallels between this story of Elijah and John's experiences with Herod Antipas and his unlawful wife, Herodias, are extraordinary. When Jesus' disciples ask him why Elijah did not come before the Messiah, twice Jesus explains that Elijah did indeed come first but no one recognized him. The first incident came while John was in prison. Jesus was speaking about John's greatness and then said in Matthew 11:14–15: "And if you care to accept it, he is Elijah, who was to come. He who has ears to hear, let him hear." The second time was after the Transfiguration in Matthew 17:12–13; Jesus explains: "Elijah is coming and will restore all things; but I say to you, that Elijah already came, and they did not recognize him, but did to him whatever they wished. Then the disciples understood that He had spoken to them about John the Baptist." John was the soul and spirit of Elijah reincarnated. Curiously, Herodias, the one who had John beheaded, may have been the reincarnation of Jezebel, who hated Elijah and swore that she would get even with him for killing her prophets of Baal (1 Kings 19:2). Head chopping would not have been new to Herodias' soul, for, as Jezebel, she had so many heads of the prophets of Jehovah chopped off that Obadiah had to "hide a hundred prophets in caves" to keep her from finding them too. Some believe that Elijah karmically "lost his head" when he exceeded his God–given assignment of proving the true God's presence to the people and priests of Baal, when, after sufficiently proving it by calling down fire from heaven to the altar, he then decided *on his own* to slay all the Baal priests (1 Kings 18:40)—something God had not directed him to do. Subsequently, Elisha replaces Elijah as God's prophet, because Elijah fears for his life by the hand of the revengeful Jezebel. So often in our zeal to spread the light, we slay former opponents on the very day we convert them; as did Elijah. In some ways, John's harsh message like Elijah's brutal action against Jezebel may have given him into her hands as Herodias, the reincarnation of Jezebel. Once Herod Antipas arrested John, he made the mistake of promising anything she wanted if Herodias' daughter would dance sensually for him. She did, and her fulling–promise request was John's head on a platter! Even though Herod did not want to do this, he felt that he was obligated and had John beheaded. Another interesting issue with Elijah, which may shed more light on John's disposition and why Jesus called him the greatest ever born of woman but the *least* in the kingdom of heaven (Matthew 11:11), is found in Elijah's comments to God about how he is the only one left in Israel who seeks God rather than Baal, to which God replies that "seven thousand in Israel have *not* bent their knee to Baal or kissed his image." (I Kings 14–18) At this point, Elijah's ministry ends and Elisha takes over. In this present incarnation John's ministry ends at the hands of Herodias and Jesus' begins.

However, John's brief ministry set the stage for Jesus'. In a dramatic speech to the Sadducees who come out to him to be baptized, John foreshadows the one who is coming in Matthew 3:10–12: "Even now the ax lies at the root of the trees. Therefore, every tree that doesn't bring forth good fruit is cut down, and cast into the fire. I indeed baptize you in water for repentance, but he who comes after me is mightier than I, whose shoes I am not worthy to carry. He will baptize you in the Holy Spirit. His winnowing fork is in his hand, and he will thoroughly cleanse his threshing floor. He will gather his wheat into the barn, but the chaff he will burn up with unquenchable fire." John explains that he had been told by the Lord that he would know the Messiah by a sign. This is in John 1:30–36: "The next day, he [John] saw Jesus coming to him, and said, 'Behold, the Lamb of God, who takes away the sin of the world! This is he of whom I said, "After me comes a man who is preferred before me, for he was before me." I didn't know him, but for this reason I came baptizing in water: that he would be revealed to Israel.' John testified, saying, 'I have seen the Spirit descending like a dove out of heaven, and it remained on him. I didn't recognize him, but he who sent me to baptize in water, he said to me, "On whomever you will see the Spirit descending, and remaining on him, the same is he who baptizes in the Holy Spirit." I have seen, and have testified that this is the Son of God.'"

As powerful as this passage is, it does have one peculiar element: John says that "he didn't know him" and that he "didn't recognize him." Since we know John and Jesus' mothers were cousins and had their sons at about the same time and that these two boys went into Egypt together, what is John saying? Perhaps the answer is that Jesus, for all his divinity, appeared perfectly normal and human on the outside. Cayce's readings confirm this. The boy Jesus was normal in every sense of the term. Therefore, John knew Jesus but did not grasp that he was the Son of God incarnate until God revealed it to him at the baptism: "And John bore witness, 'I saw the Spirit descend as a dove from heaven, and it remained on him. I myself did not know him; but he [God] who sent me to baptize with water said to me, "He on whom you see the Spirit descend and remain, this is he who baptizes with the Holy Spirit." And I have seen and have borne witness that this is the Son of God.'" (John 1: 32–34)

Jesus' Ministry

After his sojourn in Egypt to avoid being caught in Herod's decree, Jesus, now a man, returned to the Holy Land. He found John baptizing along the Jordan River and asked John to baptize him. John replied, "I need to be baptized by you, and you come to me?" But Jesus, revealing his own sense of humility and propriety, requested that John "allow it now, for this is the fitting way for us to fulfill all righteousness." Thus John baptized Jesus. When Jesus came up out of the water, the Gospels record that "the heavens were opened to him. He saw the Spirit of God descending as a dove, and coming on him." He, and apparently those around him, also heard a voice out of the heavens saying, "This is my beloved Son, with whom I am well pleased." After this momentous event it must have been surprising that the Spirit of God led him out into the desert to be tempted by the devil, as recorded in the Gospels.

In the desert Jesus fasted for forty days. When hunger became acute, he sought something to eat. At that moment the tempter appeared and delivered the first of three tests: "If you are the Son of God, command that these stones become bread." Jesus, his human side in real need of bread, took hold of a higher perspective from a time long ago when the people were sorely hungry and God fed them with manna from heaven, recalling a quote from Deuteronomy 8:3: "It is written, 'Man shall not live by bread alone, but by every word that proceeds out of the mouth of God.'" Gratifying of physical needs and wants takes a lower priority than maintaining the right perspective on one's relationship to, and trust in, God. But the devil can quote scripture, too, so he took Jesus to the Holy City and sat him on the pinnacle of the Great Temple (presumably this occurred in spirit). Then the tempter challenged him: "If you are the Son of God, throw yourself down, for it is written, 'He will give his angels charge concerning you.' And, 'On their hands they will bear you up, so that you don't dash your foot against a stone.'" Both are quotes from Psalm 91:11. To this temptation Jesus countered, "Again, it is written, 'You shall not test the Lord, your God,'" which is a quote from

Deuteronomy 6:16: "You shall not put the Lord your God to the test." Here Jesus affirms faith and patience, trusting God and the promises, no matter how seemingly impossible they appear to be, rather than demanding signs and proofs from God. Finally, the devil took Jesus to an exceedingly high mountain and showed him "all the kingdoms of the world and their glory." The tempter said to him, "I will give you all of these things, if you will fall down and worship me." To this temptation Jesus gave his strongest response, a command: "Get behind me, Satan! For it is written, 'You shall worship the Lord your God, and him only shall you serve.'" Which is another quote from Deuteronomy, 6:13–14: "You shall fear [reverence] the Lord your God; and him shall you serve, and shall swear by his name. You shall not go after other gods, of the gods of the peoples who are round about you." This reply affirms one of the most important principles of modern faiths: One God. And it gives a singleness of mind and action that is so important to fully realizing the spiritualization process in human life.

After this, the tempter leaves Jesus, and the Gospels tell us that angels came and ministered to his needs. When one's priorities are in the right order, all the powers of heaven engage with us in our lives.

At this point in Jesus' readiness to begin his ministry, his fellow teacher and baptizer, John, is arrested and put into prison by Herod Antipas. Jesus then withdrew into the region of Galilee. After visiting Nazareth, his childhood town, he lived in Capernaum, which is by the Sea of Galilee, in the region of Zebulun and Naphtali. The Gospels say that this fulfilled Isaiah's prophecy: "The land of Zebulun and the land of Naphtali, toward the sea, beyond the Jordan, Galilee of the Gentiles, the people who sat in darkness saw a great light, to those who sat in the region and shadow of death, to them light has dawned." (Isaiah 9:1–2)

The Gospels record that in this region Jesus began to preach, saying, "Repent! For the Kingdom of Heaven is at hand." Around the Sea of Galilee he began to gather his disciples, telling the fishermen broth- ers, Peter and Andrew, "Come with me and I will make you fishers for men." Initially, he gathered around himself twelve disciples. The Gospel of Matthew identifies them: "The first, Simon, who is called Peter; An- drew, his brother; James the son of Zebedee; John, his brother; Philip; Bartholomew [or, Nathanael, in John 1:42]; Thomas; Matthew the tax collector [publican]; James the son of Alphaeus; and Lebbaeus, whose surname was Thaddaeus [or, Judas, in Jude 1]; Simon the Canaanite; and Judas Iscariot, who also betrayed him."

Jesus gave these twelve "authority over unclean spirits, to cast them out, and to heal every disease and every sickness." The twelve are referred to as "apostles," from the Greek *apostello*, which means "to send forth" or "to dispatch," which is exactly what Jesus did. Matthew records their directive from Jesus as follows (Matthew 10): "Jesus sent these twelve out, and charged them, saying, 'Don't go among the Gentiles, and don't enter into any city of the Samaritans. Rather, go to the lost sheep of the house of Israel. As you go, preach, saying, "The Kingdom of Heaven is at hand!" Heal the sick, cleanse the lepers, and cast out demons. Freely you received, so freely give. Don't take any gold, nor silver, nor brass in your money belts. Take no bag for your journey, neither two coats, nor shoes, nor staff; for the laborer is worthy of his food. Into whatever city or village you enter, find out who in it is worthy; and stay there until you go on. As you enter into the household, greet it. If the household is worthy, let your peace come on it, but if it isn't worthy, let your peace return to you. Whoever doesn't receive you, nor hear your words, as you go out of that house or that city, shake off the dust from your feet. Most assuredly I tell you, it will be more tolerable for the land of Sodom and Gomorrah in the day of judgment than for that city.'"

Then he warned them: "Behold, I send you out as sheep in the midst of wolves. Therefore be wise as serpents, and harmless as doves. But beware of men: for they will deliver you up to councils, and in their synagogues they will scourge you. Yes, and you will be brought before governors and kings for my sake, for a testimony to them and to the Gentiles. But when they deliver you up, don't be anxious about how or what you will say, for it will be given you in that hour what you will say. For it is not you who speak, but the Spirit of your Father who speaks in you."

He then describes what the circumstances are: "Brother will deliver up brother to death, and the father his child. Children will rise up against parents, and cause them to be put to death. You will be hated by all men for my name's sake, but he who endures to the end will be saved. But when they persecute you in this city, flee into the next, for most assuredly I tell you, you will not have gone through the cities of Israel, until the Son of Man has come. A disciple is not above his teacher, nor a servant above his lord. It is enough for the disciple that he be like his teacher, and the servant like his lord. If they have called the master of the house Beelzebul [meaning "Lord of the House," not Beelzebub], how much more those of his household! Therefore don't be afraid of them, for there is nothing covered that will not be revealed; and hidden that will not be known. What I tell you in the darkness, speak in the light; and what you hear whispered in the ear, proclaim on the housetops."

Then he comforts and encourages them saying, "Don't be afraid of those who kill the body, but are not able to kill the soul. Rather, fear him who is able to destroy both soul and body in Gehenna (Hell). Aren't two sparrows sold for an assarion [one tenth of a drachma or a few cents in U.S. funds]? Not one of them falls on the ground apart from your Father's will, but the very hairs of your head are all numbered. Therefore don't be afraid. You are of more value than many sparrows. Everyone therefore who confesses me [the Spirit of God speaking through him] before men, him I will also confess before my Father who is in heaven. But whoever denies me [the Spirit of God speaking through him] before men, him I will also deny before my Father who is in heaven."

Now he touches on a defining issue. Is Jesus a prophet of peace and happiness, of prosperity and comfort? Or is he a prophet of change, of a struggle that calls all humans to reach new heights of faith, consciousness, spirituality, and love? "Don't think that I came to send peace on the earth. I didn't come to send peace, but a sword. For I came to set a man at odds against his father, and a daughter against her mother, and a daughter-in-law against her mother-in-law. A man's foes will be those of his own household. He who loves father or mother more than me [the Spirit of God speaking through him] is not worthy of me; and he who loves son or daughter more than me isn't worthy of me. He who doesn't take up his cross and follow after me, isn't worthy of me. He who finds his life will lose it; and he who loses his life for my sake will find it. He who receives you receives me, and he who receives me receives him who sent me. He who receives a prophet in the name of a prophet will receive a prophet's reward: and he who receives a righteous man in the name of a righteous man will receive a righteous man's reward. Whoever gives one of these little ones just a cup of cold water to drink in the name of a disciple, most assuredly I tell you he will in no way lose his reward."

Jesus' message was a message for those who were not satisfied, who were hoping, longing, seeking a better way, and not just a better material life but a more enlightened life. He reveals these in his famous beatitudes: "Blessed are the poor in spirit, for theirs is the Kingdom of Heaven. Blessed are those who mourn, for they shall be comforted. Blessed are the meek, for they shall inherit the earth. Blessed are those who hunger and thirst after righteousness, for they shall be filled. Blessed are the merciful, for they shall obtain mercy. Blessed are the pure in heart, for they shall see God. Blessed are the peacemakers, for they shall be called children of God. Blessed are those who have been persecuted for righteousness' sake, for theirs is the Kingdom of Heaven. Blessed are you when people reproach you, persecute you, and say all kinds of evil against you falsely, for my sake [the Spirit of God speaking through him]. Rejoice, and be exceedingly glad, for great is your reward in heaven. For that is how they persecuted the prophets who were before you." Notice here that the prophets also declared that it was the Spirit of the Lord that spoke to them and through them.

One of the greatest indications of Jesus' values is revealed to us when the imprisoned John the Baptist sends two of his disciples to ask Jesus if he is indeed the hoped-for Messiah. One has to wonder how John could ask such a question, after seeing the signs of Jesus' calling in Egypt and again during and after baptizing him. It goes to show just how difficult it is for our human side to keep hold of the spiritual blessings and signs we have received, especially when the physical presses hard against us, as it was for John in prison. Jesus chooses to answer John's inquiry by listing the activities that *indicate* the presence of God's Spirit. They are *not* the mighty things that impress men but the quiet, personal, loving things that reveal the true nature of our Maker and His relationship with us: "Go and tell John the things which you hear and see: the blind receive their sight, the lame walk, the lepers are cleansed, the deaf hear, the dead are raised up, and the poor have good news preached to them. Blessed is he who finds no occasion for stumbling in me."

In a prayer conversation with God, Jesus provides us with more insight into his views and mission and the nature of God's way: "I thank you, Father, Lord of heaven and earth, that you hid these things from the wise and understanding, and revealed them to infants. Yes, Father, for so it was well-pleasing in your sight. All things have been delivered to me by my Father. No one knows the Son, except the Father; neither does anyone know the Father, except the Son, and he to whom the Son desires to reveal him. Come to me, all you who labor and are heavily burdened, and I will give you rest. Take my yoke upon you, and learn from me, for I am gentle and lowly in heart; and you will find rest for your souls. For my yoke is easy, and my burden is light."

Jesus went around doing good, preaching goodness and the need to prepare for the kingdom of heaven. He taught in the countryside, in the synagogues, at social occasions, and in debates with the authorities. He taught individuals and small groups privately as well as publicly.

Prophecy of His Return

There are prophecies of the return of the Son of man, the Son of God, and of Jesus. Whether these are all the same is often debated. Some believe that the return will be as a worldwide spirit or consciousness touching everyone on the planet. Consider this description given by Jesus: "And then shall appear the sign of the Son of man in heaven; and then shall all the tribes of the earth mourn, and they shall see the Son of man coming in the clouds of heaven with power and great glory. And he shall send his angels with a great sound of a trumpet, and they shall gather together his elect from the four winds, from one end of heaven to the other." (Matthew 24:30-31) If this is to occur from "one end of heaven to the other," it would seem to be more than a single, physical being. Add to this Jesus' teaching to Nicodemus: "No one has ascended into heaven, but he who descended out of heaven, even the Son of Man, who is in heaven.'" (John 3:13) Notice in this last sentence stating that Jesus, the Son of man, though physically standing before Nicodemus, is already "in heaven." This indicates that heaven may also be a state of consciousness and can be accessed at anytime from anywhere if the mind and heart of one is tuned into or conscious of heaven's essence. And if this is so, then perhaps in reverse heaven can impact every mind and heart. Then this would explain how "all the tribes of the earth" will be impacted by the coming of Son of man "one end of heaven to the other." The veil will opened to every mind and heart and they will become conscious of this worldwide change.

Here's another Cayce discourse that adds to our understanding:

(Q) What is the meaning and significance of the words Jesus and Christ as should be understood and applied by these entities in the present?

(A) Jesus is the man—the activity, the mind, the relationships that He bore to others. Yea, He was mindful of friends, He was sociable, He was loving, He was kind, He was gentle. He grew faint, He grew weak—and yet gained that strength that He has promised, in becoming the Christ, by fulfilling and overcoming the world! Ye are made strong—in body, in mind, in soul, and purpose—by that power in Christ. The *power*, then, is in the Christ. The *pattern* is in Jesus. (2533-7)

And another: "*Christ* is not a man! *Jesus* was the man; Christ the messenger. Christ in all ages, Jesus in one. (991-1)

Here is Edgar Cayce on the return of Jesus:

Asked, "How will Jesus come again?" The Cayce readings affirm the second coming of Jesus with these words: "He shall come as you have seen him go, in the body he occupied in Galilee." (5749-4) Clearly Cayce sees a literal return in the same physical body. This is not reincarnation.

Cayce often stated in his readings that "the day of the Lord is indeed at hand." When asked how soon the second coming will be, Cayce responded: "When those that are his have made the way clear, passable, for him to come." (262-49) "(Q) What is meant by 'the day of the Lord is near at hand'? (A) That as has been promised through the prophets and the sages of old, the time and half time has been and is being fulfilled in this day and generation, and that soon there will again appear in the earth that one through whom many will be called to meet those that are preparing the way for His day in the earth. The Lord, then, will come, 'even as ye have seen him go.'" (262-49)

"He shall come as ye have seen Him go, in the *body* He occupied in Galilee. The body that He formed, that was crucified on the cross, that rose from the tomb, that walked by the sea . . .'" (5749-4)

Universal Christ

Given Edgar Cayce's Christian upbringing and annual Bible study, it is surprising how universal his amazing psychic readings are. Compared to Christian theological teachings, Cayce's readings are profoundly open to all who seek God and love their fellowman. In one of the "Work Readings" (254-92), which were given to guide the A.R.E.'s formation and management, Cayce's readings convey that there is only oneness on the other side, and the "Universal Christ-Consciousness" is the more ideal way to carry the message and the work to the world. Cayce said, "Do not consider for a moment that an individual soul-entity passing from the earth plane as a Catholic, a Methodist, an Episcopalian, is something else because he is dead! He's only a dead Episcopalian, Catholic or Methodist. For all are under the law of God equal, and how did He say even as respecting the home? 'They are neither married nor given in marriage in the heavenly home but are one!' Hence the ideals and the purposes of the Association for Research & Enlightenment are not to function as another schism or ism. Keep away from that! For these warnings have been given again and again. Less and less of personality, more and more of God and Christ in the dealings with others."

Cayce's guiding principle is all are equal under God's law. In this next reading he is quite clear about this:

> Whether they be Greek, Parthenian, Jew or Gentile—whether they be of Mohammed, Confucius, or even Shinto or On or Mu—the Lord, the God, is *one!* For all force, all power that is manifested in yourself, is of the *one* source.   1494-1

> None is convinced that scientific or religious convictions are one. The first lesson for six months should be *One*—One—One—*One*; Oneness of God, oneness of man's relation, oneness of force, oneness of time, oneness of purpose, *Oneness* in every effort—Oneness—Oneness!   900-429

> The *essence*, the truth, the *real* truth is *One*—mercy and justice; peace and harmony. For without Moses and his leader Joshua (that was bodily Jesus) there is no Christ. *Christ* is not a man! *Jesus* was the man; Christ the messenger; Christ in all ages, Jesus in one, Joshua in another, Melchizedek in another; these be those that led Judaism! These be they that came as that child of promise, as to the children of promise; and the promise is in thee, that ye lead as He has given thee, "Feed my sheep."   991-1

In this next reading, Cayce reveals how timeless Christ is:

In giving to these, then, that seek to know more of those circumstances, those conditions as surrounded that you call the first Christmas: Do not confuse yourselves. While to you it may be a first Christmas, if it were the first then there would be a last; and you would not worship, you would not hold to that which passes away. For time never was when there was not a Christ and not a Christ-mass. 262-103

Living in time makes it difficult for us to grasp that Christ and Christ's mass have always existed. In other readings Cayce expresses how each day the "babe" is born in us as we live with ourselves and among others: speaking, thinking, and doing. Whenever we speak, think, and act in harmony with the spirit of Christ (which is "love one another"), we give birth and growth to the babe within us.

He is the babe in your heart, in your life; to be nourished. For not by might nor in power, but in the still small voice that speaks within, you may know as He has given so often: "Peace, it is I! Be not afraid, it is I," your Savior, your Christ; yes, yourself meeting that Babe in your inner self that may grow even as He to be a channel of blessings to others! 262-103

Our holy babe within us, our beautifully spiritual self awaits our love and seeks more of the spiritual than the material, more of the better self than the little selfish self. Cayce said that Jesus had a personal prayer that he repeated over and over to keep him in the right frame of mind about his higher role and the higher love: "Others, Lord, others." Instead of seeking his ways, his wants, he strove to be a channel of blessings to others—whether they were a Roman centurion, a wealthy member of the Sanhedrin, or a common, everyday person—sinner or saint.

Cayce picks up on this in this next reading when he touches on the universal law of karma.

As you give so do you receive. As He has given, the love of the Father to the children of men is manifested in that spirit of Christmas—Christ-mass—that which may now be raised to that consciousness, that level above man's way of thought, man's concept of force, power or might; and that the real strength, the real hope, the real contribution is in that still small voice within. It is not in the tempest, not in the roar or the lore of the might of battle. Though there may be the destruction of life, of property—no one can destroy the soul but self! No one but self! God has not willed that any soul should perish, but has given even His Son, that brought even into the world that spirit of Christmas.   281-59

Since Cayce, a protestant, keeps using the Catholic term *mass*, let's consider what a mass is. And keep in mind, Catholicism takes many of its basic practices from the early followers of Christ, who called themselves "The Way," not Catholics.

The English word mass comes from the Latin word *missa*, which means to dismiss. The early Christian worship services ended with the congregation celebrating communion together. However, before the communion began, those who were not yet members of the congregation were dismissed. This is perhaps why the communion service came to be known as the dismissal (*missa*). Or it may be because, at the end of communion, the presiding leader would say, *Ite missa est*, meaning "you are dismissed." Either way, the term had become a common synonym for communion. In music, a mass does not mean a communion service, but rather a musical rendition of the six ancient hymns—the Kyrie, Gloria, Nicene Creed, Holy Holy Holy, Hosanna or Benedictus, and Lamb of God. Musical masses were written by both Catholic composers, like Palestrina, and Protestant composers, like Bach (Lutheran). These six hymns date at least as far back as the first century after Christ's Ascension.

Communion is the reenactment of Jesus' offering of his body and blood (or physical life) for the spiritual salvation of others—a model that each of us is to follow in loving others more than ourselves (not to an extreme; Cayce always taught "balance"). The offering is symbolized by using bread for the body and wine for the blood. In the Scriptures, this offering becomes a memorializing ceremony to celebrate this theme or ideal. As Jesus taught, "Greater love has no one than this, that he lay down his life for his friends." (John 15:13) Cayce states it this way: "Crucify desire in self; that you may be awakened to the real abilities of helpfulness that lie within your grasp." (2475-1) Less and less of self brings greater channeling of God's wisdom and love through us to those we meet and share life with.

You can see how anyone anywhere in the world could be channeling the Universal Christ Consciousness by seeking to be of help to others rather than self-seeking. Thus, the Christ message, the Christ mission, may be functioning through people of any religion, race, age, gender, ethnicity, and so on. As Jesus warned us Christians: "Other sheep I have, which are not of this fold; them also I must bring, and they shall hear my voice; and they shall become one flock, one shepherd." (John 10:16) Oneness is Godly and love is the way to Oneness.

A.R.E. PRESS

Edgar Cayce (1877–1945) founded the non-profit Association for Research and Enlightenment (A.R.E.) in 1931, to explore spirituality, holistic health, intuition, dream interpretation, psychic development, reincarnation, and ancient mysteries—all subjects that frequently came up in the more than 14,000 documented psychic readings given by Cayce.

Edgar Cayce's A.R.E. provides individuals from all walks of life and a variety of religious backgrounds with tools for personal transformation and healing at all levels—body, mind, and spirit.

A.R.E. Press has been publishing since 1931 as well, with the mission of furthering the work of A.R.E. by publishing books, DVDs, and CDs to support the organization's goal of helping people to change their lives for the better physically, mentally, and spiritually.

In 2009, A.R.E. Press launched its second imprint, 4th Dimension Press. While A.R.E. Press features topics directly related to the work of Edgar Cayce and often includes excerpts from the Cayce readings, 4th Dimension Press allows us to take our publishing efforts further with like-minded and expansive explorations into the mysteries and spirituality of our existence without direct reference to Cayce specific content.

A.R.E. Press/4th Dimension Press
215 67th Street
Virginia Beach, VA 23451

Learn more at EdgarCayce.org. Visit ARECatalog.com to browse and purchase additional titles.

ARE PRESS.COM

Who Was Edgar Cayce?
Twentieth Century Psychic and Medical Clairvoyant

Edgar Cayce (pronounced Kay-Cee, 1877-1945) has been called the "sleeping prophet," the "father of holistic medicine," and the most-documented psychic of the 20th century. For more than 40 years of his adult life, Cayce gave psychic "readings" to thousands of seekers while in an unconscious state, diagnosing illnesses and revealing lives lived in the past and prophecies yet to come. But who, exactly, was Edgar Cayce?

Cayce was born on a farm in Hopkinsville, Kentucky, in 1877, and his psychic abilities began to appear as early as his childhood. He was able to see and talk to his late grandfather's spirit, and often played with "imaginary friends" whom he said were spirits on the other side. He also displayed an uncanny ability to memorize the pages of a book simply by sleeping on it. These gifts labeled the young Cayce as strange, but all Cayce really wanted was to help others, especially children.

Later in life, Cayce would find that he had the ability to put himself into a sleep-like state by lying down on a couch, closing his eyes, and folding his hands over his stomach. In this state of relaxation and meditation, he was able to place his mind in contact with all time and space—the universal consciousness, also known as the super-conscious mind. From there, he could respond to questions as broad as, "What are the secrets of the universe?" and "What is my purpose in life?" to as specific as, "What can I do to help my arthritis?" and "How were the pyramids of Egypt built?" His responses to these questions came to be called "readings," and their insights offer practical help and advice to individuals even today.

The majority of Edgar Cayce's readings deal with holistic health and the treatment of illness. Yet, although best known for this material, the sleeping Cayce did not seem to be limited to concerns about the physical body. In fact, in their entirety, the readings discuss an astonishing 10,000 different topics. This vast array of subject matter can be narrowed down into a smaller group of topics that, when compiled together, deal with the following five categories: (1) Health-Related Information; (2) Philosophy and Reincarnation; (3) Dreams and Dream Interpretation; (4) ESP and Psychic Phenomena; and (5) Spiritual Growth, Meditation, and Prayer.

Learn more at EdgarCayce.org.

What Is A.R.E.?

Edgar Cayce founded the non-profit Association for Research and Enlightenment (A.R.E.) in 1931, to explore spirituality, holistic health, intuition, dream interpretation, psychic development, reincarnation, and ancient mysteries—all subjects that frequently came up in the more than 14,000 documented psychic readings given by Cayce.

The Mission of the A.R.E. is to help people transform their lives for the better, through research, education, and application of core concepts found in the Edgar Cayce readings and kindred materials that seek to manifest the love of God and all people and promote the purposefulness of life, the oneness of God, the spiritual nature of humankind, and the connection of body, mind, and spirit.

With an international headquarters in Virginia Beach, Va., a regional headquarters in Houston, regional representatives throughout the U.S., Edgar Cayce Centers in more than thirty countries, and individual members in more than seventy countries, the A.R.E. community is a global network of individuals.

A.R.E. conferences, international tours, camps for children and adults, regional activities, and study groups allow like-minded people to gather for educational and fellowship opportunities worldwide.

A.R.E. offers membership benefits and services that include a quarterly body-mind-spirit member magazine, Venture Inward, a member newsletter covering the major topics of the readings, and access to the entire set of readings in an exclusive online database.

Learn more at EdgarCayce.org.